THE
GOLD
RUSH...

THE GOLD RUSH

★ ★ ★ ★

*Letters from the Wolverine
Rangers to the Marshall,
Michigan, Statesman
1849-1851*

THE CUMMING PRESS

Mount Pleasant   Michigan

❧ *Introduction* ❧

Marshall, Michigan, located midway across the southern part of the state, was only eighteen years removed from the wilderness in 1849; yet it was a thriving community which boasted sawmills, furniture factories, foundries, a thrashing machine manufacturer, two newspapers, and a long list of other enterprises. From the time when George Ketchum in 1831 built the first house within the bounds of the present city, Marshall promoters envisioned a prosperous and successful future.

In the first few years of its existence, the village had engaged in a contest with Battle Creek and Kalamazoo to have itself declared the head of steamboat navigation on the Kalamazoo River. It is recorded that a lithograph view of steamboats unloading at wharves along the river was prepared by an artist; purely imaginary, for the river turned out to be too narrow and too shallow for navigation by boats of any size practical for shipping cargoes down the river to Lake Michigan.

As early as 1835 the town's promoters had set their sights on procuring the state capitol for Marshall; and so optimistic were they that they set aside land for that purpose, and an eminence within the village was designated "Capitol Hill." At first Michigan's capitol was in Detroit; but all agreed that it should someday be moved to a more central location. Marshall leaders lobbied vigorously for the honor and claimed that they had the support of leaders from other communities in the state. But this dream, too, soon vanished when a decade

[i]

later the legislature voted to move the capitol to what is present-day Lansing.

The agitation for securing the capitol for Marshall, however, is credited with having attracted a number of leading attornies, professional people, and merchants to the village in its early years.

George Ketchum, who joined another Marshall company for the overland journey to California in 1850, built the first house in what was to become Marshall in April 1831. By fall he had also built a sawmill and had moved his family from Rochester, New York, to his new home in the wilderness.

On August 26, 1831, the village plat was surveyed; and a few days later it was registered. The influx of settlers over the next few years was large, consisting principally of immigrants from New York State and New England. Spirited promotion in an era of frenzied speculation created a prosperous community in a few years. Today, the large, attractive homes of the City of Marshall attract many tourists and students of architecture. Most of them are represented in the book *Nineteenth Century Homes of Marshall, Michigan,* published by the Marshall Historical Society in 1971. A good portion of the homes represented in this book date from this early period; and some of them even today would qualify as mansions. That these homes were built within fifteen years of the first settlement is ample testimony of the prosperity which the village enjoyed in its infant years.

Sidney Ketchum, brother of George, the first settler, was the initial promoter of Marshall. It was he who first made land entries in 1830 and envisioned the bright future for his town. The Territorial Road, planned to cross the state, connected Marshall with Jackson to the east and would ultimately be extended to the west, terminating at St. Joseph, on Lake Michigan. Then agitation started in 1840 for the railroad, which finally reached Marshall on August 10, 1844.

In the meantime the financial panic which seized the

nation in the late thirties was particularly severe in Michigan, where "wildcat" banks failed and many people went insolvent, among them Sidney Ketchum. The era of unrestrained land speculation was stalled, and dreams of wealth for many vanished.

When, in 1848, the news of the discovery of gold in California reached Marshall, the dreams were awakened once again. Some saw the news as a means of restoring themselves to the stations they had once enjoyed; and others saw it as an opportunity to gain the fortune that had previously eluded them. The era of land speculation in Michigan with its paper towns and the influence of Eastern investors had had all of the elements of the gold rush. The same dreams and expectations were soon re-activated. A trial run in the form of mineral discoveries, copper and iron, in the Upper Peninsula of Michigan had already been experienced, with three companies being formed in Marshall in 1846. But this type of mining was one that required capital, while the California gold was there waiting to be picked up from the river bed by anyone.

One of the first men to succumb to the "gold fever' was James Pratt, editor of the *Marshall Statesman*, a factor which perhaps accounts for the intense interest which the discovery exerted upon the community. Pratt ran long accounts of the gold discovery in December of 1848; and on the 26th of the month he ran the following notice in his newspaper:

> The initiatory steps are being taken to raise and organize a company in this vicinity to take the overland route for California early in the Spring. An adjourned meeting of those who may wish to embark in this expedition will be held in the Editor's office next Saturday evening at 7 o'clock.

On January 3, 1949, the columns of the *Marshall Statesman* reported that two meetings had been held to discuss the possible routes to the gold fields. Two were being considered

— the Southern route via Santa Fe and the Oregon trail. It was felt that ten thousand dollars would be needed to finance such a journey. By enlisting one hundred men who would each contribute one hundred dollars the sum could be raised. Another meeting would be held on the following Friday. The newspaper of January 10th announced another meeting and stated that it would be held for the purpose of signing the articles of association and agreement of the "California Company." A ten dollar deposit would be required on signing the articles.

The next issue of the *Marshall Statesman* printed the articles of association and agreement. In them the name "Wolverine Rangers" was adopted; and each man was to agree to contribute eighty-five dollars by the twentieth of March. An agent would be sent ahead to Independence, Missouri, on March 10th to ascertain the best and cheapest manner of purchasing supplies and equipment. He would be joined by two other agents of the company in April.

Since the articles are included in this volume, it is not necessary to review them at length here. They do show that the company was being organized under intelligent leadership and that capable administrative talent was at the helm.

Nearly every community in the settled parts of Michigan was responding to the call; and companies were being organized throughout the state. The companies ranged from loosely organized, small groups of men who banded together essentially for companionship and mutual protection to the highly organized groups such as the Wolverine Rangers. At least two of the companies which started out were stock companies financed by optimistic investors who expected to share in the wealth that was certain to be picked up by the argonauts.

Captain Avery's company from Adrian, Michigan, consisted of about ten men and twenty shares. They were organized not only to make the overland trip together but also to remain intact as a company for two years. Leaving Adrian on March 15, 1849, Captain Avery's company took a somewhat different route at the start, traveling south from Toledo to Cincinnati, where they took the boat down the Ohio and all the way to St. Joseph, Missouri. Whether the investors reaped any rewards is not recorded; but Avery's company made a successful overland crossing and did remain together in the mines, at least for a time.

At about the same time a company from Monroe, Michigan, consisting of ten men set out across the state toward St. Joseph, Missouri, for the overland journey. They were backed by two men, a New York attorney and a local investor, who each put up twenty-five hundred dollars for a quarter share each in the proceeds of the company for a two-year period. Well equipped and provisioned, this company crossed the continent successfully, but not without the usual trials and hardships, however. By the time they reached California, they were no longer friends and soon parted company. It is not likely that the backers of the Monroe company realized any benefits from their investments.

The Fayette Rovers, from Hillsdale County in Michigan, started out with much attention; for this company included some of the most promising young men in the community. Although only sixteen men made up the company, they were well-organized and appeared to know what they were doing. They set Council Bluffs, Iowa, as their departure point and there joined a larger company for "mutual protection." Misfortune awaited the Fayette Rovers. Soon after their start across the plains, they experienced a series of stampedes in which they suffered a loss of a number of their oxen. Slowed down by this loss, they were forced to stop in Salt Lake City, rather than risk the late crossing of the Sierras. Here the company broke up into smaller groups.

Of all the companies which left Michigan for the gold fields in the spring of 1849, there is no question that the

Wolverine Rangers was the largest and best organized. This factor coupled with the fact that the editor of the Marshall *Statesman* was one of the promoters and leaders attracted a great deal of attention in the newspapers of the state. The company, as can be seen from an examination of the roster in this volume, drew recruits from cities and towns all across the state. The size of the company was sufficient to insure its identity; it would not be necessary for it to become a subordinate unit in a larger group.

Additional recruits continued to join the company up until the point of departure from Missouri. One William Swain, from Youngstown, Niagara County, New York, who had left his home with two friends, recorded in his diary that he had met the company from Marshall on board the boat on the Missouri and had attended services conducted by the Rev. Hobart of Marshall. A few days after landing, Swain and his companions visited the camp of the Rangers to inquire about joining the group for the overland journey. They found that by paying one hundred dollars each into the company's treasury and furnishing a wagon, they could become members. This they agreed to do.

The roster as it appeared in the Marshall *Statesman* did did not include the names of all who eventually started from that area. William Hobart, son of the Rev. Randall Hobart, is referred to in letters but is not listed on the original roster as published. Other names appear in letters from time to time; and it is not known whether all whose names were published actually went with the company.

From the start the plans and progress of the company were chronicled in the Marshall newspapers, both the *Statesman* and the *Democratic Expounder*. However, the files of the latter for most of this period have not survived, so with two exceptions the letters in this collection have been taken from the *Statesman*. One of the letters from Elmon Camp, written from Fort Laramie on July 8, 1849, was first published in the Sheboygan, Wisconsin, *Mercury,* then was reprinted by Michigan newspapers. Another letter by Elmon Camp, written from the Feather River in California on February 16, 1851, appeared in the Marshall *Democratic Expounder.* Many of the letters written home by the Wolverine Rangers excited widespread interest and were copied by newspapers throughout the state. In 1896, Oliver Goldsmith, who had accompanied the Wolverine Rangers, published an account of his experiences entitled *Overland in Forty-nine: The Recollection of a Wolverine Ranger After a Lapse of Forty-Seven Years.* One other account of the journey is known to have survived in the manuscript diary and letters of William Swain in the Western Americana Collection in the Beinecke Rare Book Library at Yale University.

James Pratt, as one of the advance agents of the Wolverine Rangers, left Marshall in the first week of March bound for Independence, Missouri, for the purpose of purchasing animals, equipment, and provisions for the rest of the company which was scheduled to rendevous at that place on April 15. Pratt's letters describing the trip in detail so that the rest of the company might be informed of the best route to Independence began to be published in the *Statesman* on March 14 and continued to appear in that newspaper in regular succession. Pratt was soon joined in Missouri by two other members of the company who were to assist him in purchasing the outfit for the overland trek. The main body of the Wolverine Rangers did not arrive at the departure point until May 2; and it was May 15 before they finally set out on the trail toward California.

The Wolverine Rangers arrived in Missouri at the height of the cholera epidemic; and news of the deaths of members of the company soon arrived in Marshall. The first victim of the scourge was Dr. Joseph H. Palmer, who had been busily engaged in treating other victims of the disease. Chauncey Nichols, a Daguerrotype artist, was next to expire. The cholera stayed with them on the trail for two weeks and took two more victims, George H. Ives on May 20, and A.S. Lyon on May 28.

Initially Jesse Baker was captain of the Wolverine Rangers; but after ten days on the trail, a reorganization meeting was held and Judge James D. Potts was elected captain, a post he retained for the balance of the trip. A spirit of comradeship seemed to prevail throughout the journey; and for the most part the Rangers made good progress. The only hint of disagreement occurred on the Fourth of July when some of the company raised objections to spending time for an observance of the holiday, rather than pushing on toward their goal. The late start and the great distance yet before them had become a source of concern for some.

At the South Pass, one of the company, John Root, recided that he could make faster progress traveling by himself, so he withdrew from the group and left alone. A few days later Oliver Goldsmith and Al Frary followed Root's example and set off by themselves with all their possessions on pack horses. Aside from these defections the rest of the group remained together until circumstances forced the dissolution of the company.

Since the first of the year, the columns of the *Statesman* had carried lengthy communications from the gold-seekers; and through these letters the friends in Marshall had been able to share the experiences of the travelers as far as the South Pass, the point the Wolverine Rangers had reached on August 1, 1849. A letter from this place by Horace Ladd appeared in the *Statesman* on September 26th. Then there was a long period of silence in the newspaper columns, broken only by a reprint of a letter from Noah Norton of Adrian, who had met with the Rangers west of the South Pass as late as August 3.

October passed without further word from the Rangers,

then November, and December. Anxiety grew in the community. The editor of the Statesman wrote in the issue of December 26:

> We have been anxiously looking for the past week for letters from some of the "Wolverine Rangers," but have been disappointed. Nothing definite can be learned of their whereabouts; but it is generally supposed that they had not arrived at the diggings on the 20th of October. Great anxiety is manifested for their welfare, by their friends in this place. We are of the opinion that they arrived there about the first of November, and that we will hear from them in about one month. And we do believe they will get there in good condition.

Word from the Wolverine Rangers finally arrived two weeks later in a letter from Horace Ladd to his wife. The party had succeeded in getting through to California, but not without great hardship. Another letter from Horace Ladd appeared in the issue of the *Statesman* on January 23, 1850; but it was not until the issue of February 20, 1850, that letters containing the details of the latter part of the trip from James Pratt and A.H. Blakesley were published.

After leaving the South Pass, Blakesley recorded, the Rangers began to have difficulty in finding feed for the cattle. The large body of emigrants who had gone before them on the trail had used up most of the grass, making it necessary for the Rangers to leave the trail and travel distances of from two to twelve miles in search of grass. Frequently they found that they had to stop to cut hay and to permit their cattle to recuperate.

Encounters with Mormon trains traveling eastward toward Salt Lake City from California warned the Rangers about further shortages of feed for the cattle and difficult terrain ahead. This factor coupled with incorrect information about trails and distances induced the Rangers to enter California through Lassen's Pass, a considerable distance farther than the Truckee route. James Pratt labeled the informants guilty of disseminating "a gross fabrication, got up expressly to bring the rear emigration into the northern settlements."

As with many other parties who chose the Lassen route, the Wolverine Rangers found the trail they had chosen to follow was not only longer but also more difficult. The approach of winter and the threat of snow in the mountain passes, a shortage of provisions, and weakened cattle, all contributed to the imminent dissolution of the well-organized company. When it became apparent that there was little hope that the company could get through intact with its wagons and equipment, a meeting was held at which it was decided to make a division of company assets and dissolve the Wolverine Rangers. Discarding most of their equipment, they then divided into smaller groups in an effort to get through to Lassen's Ranch as quickly as possible.

Fortunately all of the men survived the ordeal of the mountains. One of the survivors was Frank, a dog belonging to George Hoag. Frank had followed his master across the plains, deserts, and through the mountains. Two years later when Hoag was serving as a deputy sheriff of Butte County, Frank was still with him; and Hoag vowed that he would take his faithful friend back to Marshall with him no matter what the cost might be.

The principal correspondent of the Wolverine Rangers was James Pratt, the former editor of the *Statesman*. In addition to his letters to the Marshall newspaper, portions of his journal enitled "Notes by the Way" were published. Supplementary to Pratt's accounts were letters from Horace Ladd, Elmon S. Camp, Herman Camp, A.H. Blakesley, Rev. Randall Hobart, and Thomas E. Cook. Some of the letters were published without identification of the authors. The Charles Nash, who appears in the California letters, was a popular

Battle Creek musician who went to the gold rush in 1849 by way of Cape Horn. The letters are here published, with a single exception, that of April 4, 1849, in the order in which they appeared in the issues of the Marshall *Statesman*. From time to time this creates some flash-back and a little repetition; but after reading the letters over several times, it seemed the best way to present them.

In the spring of 1850 Elmon S. Camp for reasons of health took a trip to the Sandwich Islands and wrote a lengthy account of his observations and experiences on this voyage. Since the California gold rush exerted such a profound influence upon the future of the Hawaiian Islands, Camp's letter is considered an appropriate part of this narrative. Indeed, Camp responded to the experience with such enthusiasm that he attained heights in literary achievement unmatched in any of his other letters.

Throughout the letters the spelling as it appeared in the *Statesman* has been preserved, even when inconsistent. Double consonants appear in *waggons,* and *travellers,* and then the same words appear with single consonants. An effort has been made to preserve the original spelling. Only obvious typographical transitions have been altered. A number of California place names and words of Spanish origin are spelled as they sounded to the writers; and it is assumed that the meaning will be apparent to the reader.

The gold excitement continued to lure men, and some women from the Marshall area for several years. Large numbers left the area in 1850, 1851, and 1852. Of the Wolverine Rangers, as will be observed in reading the letters, a number of them perished in California. Some of them returned to Marshall, and others remained in California. James Pratt followed the legal profession in San Francisco until December 17, 1865, when he died at the age of 45. The Rev. Randall Hobart and his son William continued their search for gold for a number of years and were still at it during the Nevada rush in the sixties. In 1905 William Hobart served as president of the Society of California Pioneers. In 1899 Oliver Goldsmith, who had returned to Detroit, made a visit to California and renewed his acquaintanceship with William Hobart, at the time an employee of the San Francisco Water Board. The nineteen-year-old Hobart was now an "elderly, bald-headed gentleman." In Los Angeles, Goldsmith located his companion, Al Frary, who was working at a railroad depot during the winter months. In the summer he continued to return to the hills to work mining claims in hopes that he would yet strike it rich.

Special thanks is extended to the Michigan Historical Collections at the University of Michigan for permission to use its unique file of the Marshall *Statesman,* from which most of the letters in this volume were extracted.

Acknowledgment of encouragement, assistance, and advice is due Dean Russell Bidlack, University of Michigan, and Dr. Robert M. Warner, Director of the Michigan Historical Collections at the University of Michigan. William Miles, Clarke Historical Library of Central Michigan University, assisted in proof-reading and with advice; Kris Plowman provided valuable aid in typing. Archibald Hanna, Yale University; William M. Roberts, Bancroft Library; and Mrs. Virginia Rust, Huntington Library, were patient and helpful in answering inquiries. Lawrence B. Hughes, Marshall, Michigan, provided much useful information and background material; and artist Earl Nitschke drew the gold rush figure for the title page and cover. Audrey M. Cumming assisted in proofreading and countless other chores connected with the production of this book, in addition to giving the editor, printer, and publisher released time from household duties to attend the press.

There have been two meetings in this village for consultation as to the proper measures to be taken to organize a company, and as to the proper overland route to pursue to reach the glittering mines of California. It seems there are two overland routes, both starting at Fort Independence on the Missouri river, about 400 miles from St. Louis—the one, the southern route by Santa Fe, we should judge the longest, as to avoid the vast desert of the rocky mountains, a long detour is requisite to strike the Pacific at San Diego. The other overland route — called the northern — starting from the same point, Fort Independence, is the caravan route to Oregon, until Fort Hall, or one of the tributaries of the Columbia river is reached, where the emigrants for Oregon take a north-westerly, and those for California a south-westerly direction, on a route pursued by General Kearney to New Helvetia on the Sacramento river. As near as we are able to ascertain, the distance from Independence to New Helvetia, via Fort Hall is about two thousand miles. Within an hundred miles of Fort Hall, on the south lies the Great Salt Lake where the Mormons are settled, where gold is said to be abundant. A company should not start without an abundance of supplies, which can probably be purchased, including not only the teams, but the provisions and other stores, better in Missouri than here, considering the expense and wear and tear of transportation from here to Fort Independence, from which point the company should start unwearied, for the great journey beyond.

[1]

Ten thousand dollars in money to be raised by one hundred men, paying one hundred dollars each, would probably make a sum sufficient to purchase all the necessaries to reach California, and leave enough for several months subsistence after arriving there.

January 17, 1849

At a meeting of the "WOLVERINE RANGERS", held at the office of the Secretary, in Marshall, on the 13th inst., it was, on motion,

Resolved, That the publishers of the Marshall Statesman, and Democratic Expounder be requested to publish the Articles of Association and Agreement in their papers for the information of the public.

The Books of the Company are open at the office of the Secretary, where any one wishing to join can make application at any time before the first day of March next. It would be well for those who intend to go, to join as soon as convenient, so as to have a voice in the selection of the Agents of the Company, and of its officers under the articles of Association.

The present temporary officers, for the purpose of completing the organization of the Company, are, RANDALL HOBART, Chairman; JAS. PRATT, Secretary; LUCIUS G. NOYES, Treasurer.

Articles of Association and Agreement entered into, and made by the undersigned, for the purpose of mutual safety and advantage, in prosecuting an overland route to California from Independence on the Missouri River, and after arriving at the place of destination.

1st, This company shall be called the "Wolverine Rangers."

2nd, Its officers shall be a Board of five Directors, a Captain, Lieutenant, Secretary, Treasurer, and Steward, to be elected by a majority of the members.

[2]

3d, Each member shall pay into the Treasury, by the 20th day of March next, the sum of eighty five dollars in current funds—ten dollars of the above sum must be paid on signing these Articles of Association, to be forfeited in case the balance is not paid as above specified — provided, also that the Board of Directors shall have power to raise by an equal assessment upon the members an amount not exceeding in all the sum of one hundred dollars, including the eighty five dollars above the required to be paid in, should the said Directors deem it necessary to do so.

4th, By the tenth day of March next, an Agent to be selected by the Company, shall be sent to inquire into and ascertain the points where supplies can be purchased the cheapest and best — and by the first day of April, two members, to be chosen in like manner, shall be sent to join the said Agent, with the funds of the Company, and assist him in purchasing said supplies, and forwarding them to Independence, the starting point of the Company, where a settlement shall be made with the said Committee, by the Board of Directors, and submitted to the Company for their action. — the said last mentioned agents to give bonds to the satisfaction of the Director for the faithful discharge of the trust reposed in them.

5th, All supplies and property purchased with the Company funds, shall be joint property—belonging to those who start from Independence together for the route, and who there shall be considered as constituting said company. The members shall be present at Independence by the first day of May, and any person not there by the time the company leaves that place, shall forfeit all he has paid in — and have no interest in the company property — unless such person shall be reinstated by a vote of a majority of the company.

6th, After arriving at the gold regions in California, any member of the company may retire therefrom, on giving two weeks notice to the Directors, or any three of them, of his intention to do so. Whereupon the said Board of Directors shall settle with such person equitably, allowing him his share of the company avails taking his receipt, and ordering his retirement to be entered in the company record.

7th, Each member binds himself upon his honor, to fulfill as far as he can his duties as a member of this association — to be orderly, temperate and faithful — obedient to the will of the majority, properly expressed — and to stand by and relieve, so far in his power, any member in peril or distress.

8th, The Board of Directors shall hold their offices for six months — shall have charge of the expedition and the interests of the company — settle accounts — hear and adjust grievances – report monthly to the company the state of the finances, and the condition of the company affairs — recommend when necessary appropriations, draw drafts on the Treasury for such sums only as are appropriated by a majority of the company, a certificate of the Secretary of the vote, to accompany the draft. From any decision, or order of the Board, an appeal may be taken to a majority of the company by any member who may consider such appeal proper or desirable. And such Board shall report as soon as possible to the company the name of such person as may have given notice of his wish to retire from the company.

9th, The Captain shall hold his office for three months. It shall be his duty to conduct and command the expedition, pursuant to the orders and suggestions of the Board of Directors — and to preserve order and decorum on the members.

10th, The Lieutenant shall hold his office for three months — and it shall be his duty to aid and assist the Captain in the performance of his duties.

11th, The Secretary shall hold his office for six months — shall keep a record of the proceedings of the Board of Directors, and of the company — shall certify to the chairman of the Board of Directors, the vote appropriating monies for the use of the company — and do all other acts incident to his office.

12th, The Treasurer shall hold his office for three months. He shall pay all orders drawn on him by the Board of Directors, which are accompanied by a certificate of the Secretary of the vote appropriating the money — he shall report to the Board of Directors, monthly, the state of the Treasury — and shall deliver up all effects, monies and other things belonging to his office, when directed to do so by a vote of the company; and he shall give bonds to the Secretary and his successors in office in an amount to be fixed by the Board of Directors and to their satisfaction.

13th, The Steward shall hold his office for six months. He shall have charge of the provisions, and serve up and distribute the company's rations. He shall report monthly the state of his department.

It is understood that in case of the death of a member, his share of the company property shall be settled by the Board of Directors, and kept by them for his next of kin, or for those whom the deceased may have expressed a wish should receive it, and be paid over to them as soon as practicable.

Each member shall provide himself with a good rifle, 3 lbs. powder, 10 lbs. lead, and a good hatchet, and such other things as he may deem desirable, or useful.

These articles, or any of them, may be amended, and others added, by a vote of two-thirds of the members.

The Board of Directors, or a majority of them, shall have power to call meetings upon sufficient notice.

These articles shall bind the undersigned, their heirs, executors, administrators and assigns.

Mr. Editor; — I have some leisure this afternoon, and conclude to employ myself in noting some matters that may be of interest to some of your readers.

We left Niles on Monday evening in the stage, rode all night, and the next day, until evening, when, on account of bad roads, we were advised to stay all night at a log house station about 25 miles from Chicago. In our progress next day we saw the wisdom of the temporary delay; for sluices and streams had to be crossed that would have been impracticable in the night, for they were dangerous in the day-time.

We arrived at this city yesterday, at 1 o'clock P.M. It is a large city of some 20,000 inhabitants. There are some delightful residences, particularly along the beach of the lake. The river is full of shipping, and preparations are busy for early navigation, though there is much ice to be seen in the lake.

There are several splendid public houses, among them the Sherman House, and the City Hotel. I stop at the Tremont House, where every thing is got up in good style, and where a Californian can experience as much comfort, and receive as good attention, as he should have to prepare him for what is ahead!

Chicago is noted for its muddy streets; apologies and excuses are made to me for not seeing them in their glory. Yet I am satisfied with them as they stand, and would recommend those who have boots to arrange to use them here; for it is doubtful if there is any place between Marshall and "gold diggins" where they will be of more service.

There are four daily papers here; the *Journal, Democrat, Advertiser* and *Tribune,* two of them Whig, one Democrat, and one Free Soil. Including daily, weekly, and monthly papers, there are nineteen published in the city.

The Inaugural Address of Gen. Taylor gives, generally,

good satisfaction. As was expected, Old Zack has taken moderate ground, which cannot but be acceptable to all who think more of the *Union* and the national prosperity, than of mere partisanship.

An election of Mayor and Aldermen came off day before yesterday. The controversy was between the present Mayor, Mr. Woodworth, and one Wait, who received the nomination of the "Boys" and got some 300 votes, whilst Woodworth received over 2000. In a city which can boast of 23 churches, it would have been a strange occurence to have chosen "one of the b'hoys" for its chief magistrate.

The stages from the South are delayed by bad roads and high water. The Illinois and Fox rivers are twenty feet higher than usual. At Peoria, it is said the water is in many places above the windows of the houses.

I have met many bound to the El Dorado. — Those who have started in teams from the interior of Michigan will find a long and tedious journey before them to reach the Missouri. Yet they will have the experience of what they can endure; and if they do not falter in that part of the trip, the insurance agents need have no fears for them thereafter.

There will be within one hundred leave this city this spring for California. They are fitting up their wagons here, which cost them $80.00. They go in messes of four, some with oxen, others with mules or horses. I saw a drove of 22 brought from the southern part of the state yesterday. They were sent for expressly by persons going from here. They cost $65 each.

The fare from Niles to this city is five dollars, from here to Peru by stage it is the same; from Marshall to Independence this season of the year the expense will not vary much from $25.

The weather here is very fine and business seems brisk. More anon.   Yours, &c.,   J.P.

DEAR SIR: — We are now at the bridge which crosses the Du Page river at this place. We arrived last night at 12 o'clock. We journeyed from Chicago, yesterday 42 miles, through a rich prairie country, and in mud and water at the risk of flesh and blood. It is 50 miles further to Peru. The rivers and streams are high, and we have dismal accounts of the difficulties in our way. We will probably have to continue on in the stage until we reach Peoria, as it is said the boats are not yet running to Peru.

I have barely time to give you a statement of my whereabouts. We have a load of seven passengers, two Irishmen, two Yankees, (one live one, and a good specimen,) and the other 3 common men. The live Yankee makes fun enough for all. One of the Irishmen is bound for California with his gun. He got it at Chicago, having had the night before his departure a "big time" with his friends in that city. On his taking leave we had a fine exhibition of Irish feeling. He shook hands warmly with his brethren, embraced them, bade them adieu with kisses, whilst tears trickled down his roughly marked cheeks. The stage is ready and I must leave.

OTTOWA, ILL., March 13, 1849

We reached Ottowa last evening, having traveled 13 miles yesterday, and 12 miles the each two preceding days. Here the stage can go no further on account of high water. This place is situated at the confluence of the Illinois and Fox rivers. The Illinois and Michigan canal is in sight. It passes over the Fox river here and through a heavy aqueduct, supported on stone abutments and seven heavy stone pillars. There are a number of Californians here with wagons and oxen. They got here with great difficulty, and propose to send on their wagons by water, and drive their teams. Wagons can be taken by the river to St.

Louis for $1, and from there to Independence for fifty cents per 100 lbs.

This is a fine village and is said to be a delightful place in the summer. Now on account of the mud which is knee deep in the streets, it is very disagreeable. The village is well built. The business streets are in the form of a square, something as in Ann Arbor, and a large splendid Court House in an enclosure, ornamented with shade trees, stands in the centre, an ornament and an honor to the place. Ottowa contains a population of about 3,000 and is in the midst of a fertile country. It is to be a place of much importance.

A steam-boat is expected here daily, and many besides myself are awaiting its arrival with anxiety.

If you could have seen our stage load the last two days, wading over the Illinois prairies in mud and water, you would have smiled at the forlorn appearance we exhibited. I wished for a panoramic view of us, to be presented to some friends in Marshall. Sunday it rained all day, and we were completely drenched. I lost my India rubbers and with light boots proceeded on my way. I was well enough pleased however to walk three days in the rain and mud, in view of its being good preparatory exercise — not so however with my fellow travelers, for the Irishman with his gun bound for California, concluded he had "seen the Elephant" near enough, and returned to Chicago in the first stage we met. The live Yankee from this place. He is over 60 years of age, from Shefield, Massachusetts, and stands hard weather and hard fare like a young man. We are sorry to lose him as a traveling companion.

The Mansion House at Ottowa is the place to stop for any coming this way. From all I have seen I am sure we do better to purchase our wagons and teams, &c. in Missouri, even should they cost considerably more, than to undertake to drive them from Michigan.

I write to you, but cannot tell when the letter will reach

you, or even if it will leave here. It will be hard traveling until the canal opens, and then it will be quite another thing to go to Independence, from what it is now. It will be cheaper, and much more agreeable.

The high waters are somewhat abating. The rain has ceased and today it is warm and pleasant. The first boat is to come up here from Peru; so it is as well for travelers to wait here, where there are but few houses afloat, as to swim to Peru, a great part of which is inundated.

Yours,   J.P.

[April 4, 1849]   *St. Louis, March 20, 1849*

DEAR SIR: — The Steamer Tamerlon reached the city last Saturday. We had a heavy load, both of passengers and freight, and made slow progress, and had rather uncomfortable quarters. During the passage a row happened between the Captain, Roff, and the Mate, Kelly, in which the Captain was struck. He undertook to discharge the Mate, but the rest of the crew rebelled, and the Captain had to stifle his resentment. Subsequently we got along very well, with the exception of once in the night, owing to the high water in the Illinois, which covered the whole country for miles at a depth of from 5 to 10 feet, we lost the channel and floated into the woods, and were stopped by the branches of a mammoth oak. With much labor and some hazard we got out of the scrape and pursued the rest of the way without impediment or accident.

St. Louis looks beautifully from the river. — Situated on high ground, and skirted all along the levee with steamboats, one is struck with the magnitude and business capacity of the city at a glance. It is a great city, numbering 65,000 souls; and it is rapidly growing. They who have lived here the last 12 years tell of wonderful changes — how that population has trebled; and the value of property, how vastly it has appreciated.

I dropped in at the Court House, in the Rotunda, at a Democratic meeting on Saturday evening, called to express the sentiments of the democracy of St. Louis on certain resolutions recently passed by the Missouri Legislature. It is understood that Mr. Benton is to be, or is in favor of Wilmot Proviso, and the democracy here are hastening to range themselves with him on that question. He is expected here in a few days, with the intention of stumping the State, and the Nicholson letter Locofocos tremble at the result. There is a strong free soil party in Missouri, and it would not be surprising at all if Benton should take the majority of the State with him.

The city is full of strangers — principally Californians. Every boat brings fresh supplies. It is estimated that there are 3 or 4000 in the city; whilst many have taken their departure for Independence, and St. Joseph. I am to leave to-day in the Steamer *Alice*, said to be the best boat on the Missouri. I should have gone yesterday, but an old friend told me that the *Alice* will reach Independence sooner than the boats which left yesterday. The fare to Independence is $8,00.

The weather is very warm, like May. There is a good deal of sickness in the city; and it is said there have been some cases of the cholera.

I took a ride about two miles out of the city yesterday on a mule. A friend of mine, W — A — of Ithaca, N.Y., here to purchase mules, &c. for the Ithaca company, lent me an amiable, long-eared gentle animal that only wheeled once with me, whilst the one he rode kicked every way, and reared and pitched to the great amusement of men, women and children through the whole length of Market street. It is an amusing spectacle to see a man break a mule in a crowded city. Every thing alive in the vicinity of a mule's heels, makes tracks. My friend had an open passage made for him in the crowd, although he was half an hour riding the length of one square.

[11]

On each side walk 10 or 12 men kept along side of him to see and enjoy the sport. I think I had rather driven an ox than ride a mule.

Our friend D. Wallingford was taken quite sick yesterday at the City Hotel. I just came from his room; and he is still in much pain. He has good medical attendance, Dr. Frazer of this city. His disease seems to be an inflamation of the bowels.

Every thing in the way of supplies can be bought reasonably here, with the exception of fire arms. Pistols are higher here than farther east. There is a large India Rubber House here. A first rate India rubber coat costs $8,00, overalls 3,50, carpet bag 3,50. Overalls with feet for boots $7,00.

As I leave this afternoon have but little time to write.

Yours, &c   J.P.

————————⟨◆⟩————————

[April 25, 1849]   INDEPENDENCE, *Miss., April 3, 1849*

I arrived here one week ago last evening, and am boarding with several others about a mile from town, and walk in every day.

This is quite a large village, and there are two landings, the lower landing is about six miles from the village, and the Wayne city landing ten miles farther up the river, but only three miles from the village. It is at the latter landing we stopped. Independence is a busy town. The Court House Square is the centre of the business part of the place, and is the theatre for trade. It is surrounded every day with horses, oxen, mules and ponies for trading, and it is very interesting to watch the movements of the traders. There have been several parties in from Santa Fe since I came here, and I am satisfied, on seeing many who have been over the plains, that I can perform the trip without much danger or difficulty.

There are many parties here from different parts of the

country already, encamped out in the neighboring openings. Men arriving here stop but a short time at the public houses, for they charge $5 a week, and good accommodations can be had in the neighborhood for $2. The weather is warm, the grass green, and the probability is that the emigrants will be able to leave about the 20th inst.

. . . . . . is expecting the . . . . . . company here daily — they are to go with packed mules, and will get along faster than we do with oxen. I am waiting here for . . . . . . to come from St. Louis and help me buy the oxen, and have ordered all our supplies except oxen and bacon to be bought in St. Louis. I intended to return to St. Louis, but concluded, after reaching here, to remain.

I stop at the plantation of Mr. Levant. There is good living here, and every thing comfortable. It is a large plantation, and quite a number of servants, who seem to enjoy themselves very well.

There is a young gentleman with us who came from St. Louis in my company, who is buying ox teams to move his mother, about 53 years of age, and 4 sisters and brothers to California. He is from Mississippi, and his family are in St. Louis, where he left them to come here to make arrangements. He had a greater responsibility than I would be willing to assume, yet I think he will get along with safety. The character of the emigration is good, and there is nothing to apprehend from that quarter.

Many of the emigrants go up the river further and start from St. Joseph and Council Bluffs.

I am very much pleased with the State of Missouri. Men seem to make more money and easier here than in Michigan, and the country is very fine and fertile. Trading is the great business of this place.

I have no misgivings as to our trip, and anticipate much pleasure in meeting . . . . . . and many other friends soon.

It would amuse you much to be here and see the Californians. Most of them let their beards grow, and their varied dresses give a picturesque appearance to the place. Mules, oxen, ponies, &c., are all the rage, and it is a real sport to see them undertake to break in the mules.

I shall feel much relieved when our company get ready to start. As soon as they get here, I presume we shall be prepared to camp out. I will write again before we leave.

DEAR SIR: I have been so much employed with the object of my mission, that I have found little opportunity to think of my engagement to keep you and your readers advised of my discoveries and whereabouts. I have now been in this village and vicinity about two weeks. The steamer *Alice*, which plies between St. Louis and St. Joseph, touching at the intermediate ports, brought us safely here. She is a fine boat, and all coming this way would do well to take her, even at a delay of several days in St. Louis. The Missouri River, is, of course, a magnificent stream, with a wide, rapid, muddy current, and it being the only water one has to drink, while upon it, the last feature becomes quite apparent. We left St. Louis Wednesday morning and arrived at the upper landing, Independence, the ensuing Sunday morning. There are two landings here, the lower within six miles of the village, and the upper within three. The upper landing is the best place of debarkation, although owing to a curve in the river it is fifteen miles further up. There are two public houses here, the Independence House, and the Noland House. — They are large, commodious, and just now very expensive to stop at. Five dollars per week is the price of board and lodging. The great body of the emigrants merely stop there, and then either at once camp out, or procure board at private houses in the neighborhood at from

$1.50 to $2.00 per week. I am boarding with some 18 others at Mr. Levants, one mile south of the village. Within a hundred rods of us is a camp of Cincinnatians, who have been enjoying the camp life for about two weeks. They have everything in fine order. They number about fifty. Their mules are in adjoining field, and it is amusing to see their endeavors to break them. Every day they hitch up a team of fresh mules, and take a ride to town. Within half a mile of us is a camp of the Kansas Indians. — The Indians within the neighborhood are all friendly. Most of the emigration goes further up the river, although this is the best place to procure stock of all kinds. It is really an interesting spectacle to go into town to see the trading go on. A large square, on which the Court is situated, occupies the centre of the business portion of the village, as is customary in many places I have seen. The streets all around are filled with ponies, mules and oxen for sale. The price of ponies varies from 35 to 60 dollars, according to the quality. Fine mules can be bo't for sixty dollars, cheaper than in St. Louis by 10 or 15 dollars. Young oxen of the medium size are recommended by all who have gone over the Plains as the best suited for the trip, and they can be bought at an average of 45 dollars per yoke. By scouring through the country and picking them up of farmers, I have been enabled to buy 20 yoke at an average of 40 dollars, which is acknowledged by all to be five dollars per yoke cheaper than any one else has purchased this spring. I took a man with me acquainted with the people, a good judge of stock, and an experienced trader, and that is the reason I succeeded so well, and not because of my talent in that kind of business.

We are having April showers and vegetation looks well. In the course of two weeks many will take up their line of march for their great journey. I hear of some who have concluded to go no farther; but they are few. There are two gambling houses here open day and night, where some of the Californians stand a good chance of being so fleeced that they can neither return home or go farther. The laws of Missouri are stringent against gambling; yet men in the face of pains and penalties pursue this hellish practice.

On Tuesday last I took a ride of about twenty miles south east looking for stock. After going nine miles through a timbered country we struck the prairies. The timber is about as thick as our oak openings, but there is more underbrush. The country all around is well watered. When upon the prairies one sees in the distance what appears to be a little fringe of shrubbery, advancing one finds timber land from half a mile to 3 miles wide. This description of woodland lines the prairies, and along it the farmers locate. For a farming state Missouri cannot be excelled. It is that peculiar institution of slavery which prevents much emigration here. At every farm house the first living thing one sees is a troup of little curly headed darkies, who seem happy enough, yet one from a non-slaveholding state cannot help regarding them with sympathy. There are about a dozen of servants or slaves, on the farm where we board. There are so many little fellows of the same size, and so much alike, that I have not undertaken to count them. Uniformly in this State, as far as I have seen, the slaves are well treated, and the farmers, although they are bitterly opposed to any thing like abolition, do not object to some system of gradual emancipation; for they know it would be better for the State if no slave darkened its soil.

Those who have come here in advance of their friends are anxiously looking for their arrival, and for letters from home. The little 7 by 9 Post Office here is crowded when open. It takes a long time to be waited upon, so great is the rush. The mail only comes tri-weekly, and by land at that, which takes 4½ days from St. Louis. I have been fortunate enough to receive papers and letters from Marshall, and they come like messengers of mercy to dispel anxious fears. One of the most serious deprivations of the route will be the total dearth in this respect, which must be endured for months. Documents to Californians after the 2d April should be addressed to New Helvetia or San Francisco. Then on arriving in California, emigrants would find there a good supply to reward them for their painful suspense.

While writing here, a young gentlemen of our mess who hails from Seneca county, and who has been in Michigan, scratched off the following for us to sing, and it is so appropriate and breathes so much of the right sentiment, I give it to you.   J.P.

AIR—*Oh Susannah don't you Cry.*

We have come from the old Empire State,
    A goodly chosen band;
We are bound for California,
    That bright and sunny land!
We have left Cayuga's pleasant shore,
    For scenes untried and strange;
The deserts barren, arid, waste,
    The prairie's boundless range!

Chorus. — Oh California!

    Thou land of glittering dreams,
        Where the yellow dust and diamonds, boys,
        Are found in all thy streams!

We've left our native woods behind,
    We've left our boyhood hills,
Where oft in school boy days we've roamed,
    Among their rocks and rills.
With quivering lip and swelling eye,
    We looked a last fond look
At home, and as we breathed "good bye,"
    Courage *almost* forsook.

    But California, &c.

We're sons of gallant fathers, boys,
    And mothers kind and true,
Who whispered as they rung our hands,

"God bless and be with you."
Wives, scores of sympathizing friends,
    Who wish us hearty speed,
Besides the *world* to back us, if
    Our steps to fortune lead.

    Thou California, &c.

Besides the boys from Tompkin's hills,
    And Seneca's bright farms,
We've e'en found one who leaves for gold,
    The burr-oak opening charms!
A "Wolverine Ranger" is he termed,
    (In truth a war-like name,)
And to become one, he forsakes
    A post well known to fame.

    Oh California, &c.

Old Mississippi too, gives us
    A scion of her blood,
Who leaves her perfumed orange groves,
    To find a wealth a flood.
For California's mountain brooks,
    For California's plain
He leaves his shady cypress groves,
    His cotton, corn and cane!

    Oh California, &c.

And all of us — have we not left
    Our best of life for this?
But cheer we up! we will return
    Laden with gold and bliss!
Then saddle our mules! away we go
    With fancy hopes by fancy led,
To where the Sacramento flows
    Over its glittering bed!

    Oh California, &c.

The Wolverine Rangers take their final leave of Marshall on Tuesday or Wednesday of next week. We have been furnished with the following list of officers and members of the company, and the residence and occupation of each, as far as could be ascertained:

Jesse J. Baker, Captain;
S.S. DeArman, Lieutenant;
George B. Allcott, Secretary;
Thomas E. Cook, Treasurer,
Herman Camp, Steward;

Board of Directors—Randall Hobart, Thos. Rawson, Horace C. Ladd, Wm. Carley, George W. Hoag.

Agents—James Pratt, J.D. Potts, Randall Hobart.

Names of Members	Residence	Occupation.
James Pratt	Marshall	Lawyer
E C Noyes	Plymouth	
James D. Potts	Marshall	Saddler
Horace C. Ladd	do	do
Thomas Manser	do	do
George W Hoag	do	Blacksmith
Jesse G Baker	do	Machinist
Randall Hobart	do	Local Preach'r
Chauncy Nichols	At Large	Daguerrean
Charles A Barton	Marshall	Carpenter
George B. Allcott	do	Student
S S De Arman	do	Tinner
Joseph Rogers	Clarendon	Farmer
Thomas Rawson	St. Joseph	Local Preach'r
L Brooks	Bellevue	Blacksmith
Almon P Frary	Lansing	
J C Climper	do	Millwright
Julius A Kent	Marshall	Clerk

Herman Camp	do	Speculator at large
J A Sutherland	do	Blacksmith
Benjamin Givin	do	Joiner
John Warren	do	Blacksmith
William Carley	Allegan	Lt. House keeper
S H McClellan	Galesburg	Farmer
William Highly	St. Joseph	
Samuel D Moore	Battle Creek	Local Preach'r
Frederick Mills	Gull Prairie	Farmer
A H Blakesly	Marshall	Tanner
Henry Gray	Hastings	
D D Fralick	Plymouth	Blacksmith
H A Bently	do	do
Joseph Henry Palmer	Vermontville	Physician
Oliver Goldsmith	Detroit	Tobaccanist
Ira Vits	Albion	Farmer
John McAlister	Battle Creek	Lawyer
George Van Brunt	Athens	Farmer
F C Cannon	Manchester	
Thomas E Cook	Marshall	Clerk
S G Noble	Unadilla	Carpenter
C B Carr	Manchester	Physician
Volney Chapman	do	Farmer
William J Magoon	do	
H B Seymour	Saugatuc	
James McCormick	Allegan	
Noah E Ives	Plainfield	
George H Ives	do	
A S Lyon	Manchester	
Thomas Delong	Lansing	
Hugh M. Phillips	Detroit	Miner
John Campbell	Manchester	
Morgan L Rood	Bellevue	Gunsmith

The emigration is fast moving off towards the Plains. Our company has not yet arrived. It will require much time and labor to prepare for marching, after they get here. We cannot be ready to start before the 10th of May. Yet I believe that is well enough, for the grass will then be just about right, and the mass of the emigrants will then be ahead of us. The Ithaca company, under charge of Dr. White, are encamped just opposite where I board, one mile south of the village. Charles Stuart is captain of their company, Dr. White being President; and he is here in command. That company will go with packed mules; but will not get ready before we do.

People are here from all the states, and many are still coming. Gov. Boggs has written another letter to his friends here — a private letter — and he tells them, no matter what may be their business, to leave immediately for California. The letter starts off a good many more from this part of the country. Gov. Boggs left the State poor, and has found an immense fortune, also several known here who went with him. So I think still we are on the right track. People living about here accustomed to life on the plains, make but little fuss about going over, otherwise than to go well provided.

There is a "Pioneer Line of Stages" here to start soon, fare $200, through in 60 days, 100 lbs. baggage is allowed.

The carriages are light, with springs, and well covered and sheltered and capable and intended for six passengers. They are light, beautiful vehicles for pleasure-riding, very different from what the uninitiated would expect to see for such a trip. There are 18 of these carriages in the line, marked in staring letters "Pioneer Line — St. Louis and San Francisco." It will not be long before a journey from Independence to San Francisco can be made as quickly as now from Boston to Independence.

Mr. Potts and myself are anxiously awaiting our company.

We are both well; and the Judge is as full of fun and humor as ever. He never allows an occasion to pass, whether among strangers or acquaintances, when there is any chance for a joke, without finding a way of cracking it.

Mr. Hall's family, the young gentleman of whom I wrote in a former letter as going to California with his mother, brothers, and four sisters, has arrived at the Landing, and he is engaged to-day in getting their goods here. They are to encamp a few days in a lot of Mr. Smarts, and will be shortly on the road. The old lady is 53 years of age, two of the sisters young ladies, two of them little girls, and then Mr. Hall and his brother, young men. They are going to travel in company with a party from Pleasant Hill, about 20 miles from here, where our cattle are now feeding. We shall also probably start from the same point and about the same time. The Pleasant Hill company consists of quite a number of families; in all there will be in that company, about 150 souls. If we travel with them it will make a large party.

From all I can judge, there will be from 12 to 15,000 people cross the Plains for the gold of Ophir this season; although there are many backing out from the expedition.

We are invited to supper this evening at 5 o'clock with Mr. Moore and Smith from Battle Creek in their camp near the village. They are young men who talked of joining us in Marshall, but who came on in their team with their supplies, and who now conclude to travel in our train.

[May 23, 1849]   INDEPENDENCE, May 5, 1849

Our company arrived here Wednesday night, the 2d inst. The same day the Judge and myself having an intimation they were approaching, rode off 20 miles on the prairies, where we were keeping our cattle, and returned with 14 yoke of them, which we thought we might have to use immediately. Thursday evening, we found Messrs. Hobart and Rawson at our boarding house waiting to see us. Brother Hobart shook hands cordially with us, and told me he [had] no need to ask me how I had been, for my appearance satisfied him on that point. Rawson said he would hardly have known me, so great was the change. And Judge Potts had to describe his meeting me when he got here. The Judge was walking along on the side walk in the village, looking for me the morning he arrived, when he said he heard some one call him by name. He said on seeing me approach him, he became alarmed, thinking it was some one going to rob him. But when I spoke again and smiled, he recognized me as the 1st agent of the Wolverine Rangers. Our company are all now in good health, a few of them I learn were sick on the route. They have landed at the lower landing, some seven miles from where I board, and in doing so they escape a high, bad hill, which would have taken us two days to surmount, with our heavy freight, and not very well broke teams. Besides this, the lower landing is a delightful spot, affording good pasturage, in the vicinity of fine farms where corn and oats can be had, and also a large magnificent warehouse, where our property is stored, and above all, the great mass of the emigration move to the upper landing, the most miserable and disagreeable place in the world. It is truly fortunate they landed where they did — they made up their minds to do so only about an hour before reaching the spot. Yesterday morning Potts, Rawson and myself walked down to the landing, 7 miles. We let Hobart ride one of the ponies — we have bought two for the company's use, in heading cattle, &c. It rained all day, and I returned from camp about 9 o'clock P.M., sore and lame. To-day, as I remarked before, I am in good order with the exception of a sore throat. I found the boys at work at the landing. Our wagons are all covered. They are very nice, light wagons, 17 of them. The boys are also making tents. There will be a tent to every mess, so we can either

[23]

sleep in our wagons or tents just as we choose. Kent had brought my things all in good order.

I had a long and interesting conversation with Col. Gilpin the other day, a young man of much distinction, familiar with the route, for he has traveled and fought for the government for years. He says we may not see an Indian on the whole route. That there is no danger. That we must place our sentinels and keep good guard, and if the Indians come up to trade or otherwise, never to admit them in the camp. But all transactions with them should be done outside the sentinels. That we should let them understand if they passed the sentinels they would be shot, and he says they will keep back. There will be, as near as I can judge, during the season from 20 to 30,000 people cross the plains. The idea of danger from [Indians] is preposterous and absurd. There is some difficulty to be be apprehended in certain localities for the want of grass and water, but we shall go provided in each wagon, with some grain for extreme cases, and with kegs &c., for water. The season is very backward here, not so far advanced I should judge from your description, as in Marshall. The emigrants are fast moving off. We shall be ready to move, I think, during the next week. Every thing seems to have favored us thus far. Our company arrived here early enough, and late enough. If they had got here earlier, it would have cost us a good deal more — if much later we might have lost some good travelling time. I had rather start next week than earlier or much later. Geo. Hoag came up with us last night, and he and the Judge drive down the cattle we had here to the landing; and I have taken to-day to rest and to write.

[May 30, 1849]   *MONDAY, May 14, 1849*

Camp 6 miles below Independence, 4 P.M.
DEAR SIR: It falls to my lot to convey to you the mourn-

ful intelligence of the death of your brother, Dr. Palmer. He died this morning at 4 o'clock of the Cholera. He was taken on Sunday morning about 4 o'clock and lived about 22 hours. He had been complaining of a looseness of the bowels ever since we left Chicago, and soon after leaving St. Louis was taken down, and he thought at that time, and has since told me, that he thought he had the cholera. He however recovered, and when we reached here was quite smart. One week ago to-day he went to Independence to buy some chemical tests and a few medicines; he stayed all that day and the next, and while there prescribed for the cholera in one case, where a man was in convulsions; he cured him in a short time; he came home in the evening and stayed with us until Thursday afternoon, when he was sent for by Mr. Moore, a gentleman from Battle Creek, bound for California. He (Mr. Moore) had the cholera, and when Dr. Palmer returned on Thursday evening, he had small hopes of his recovery; on Friday morning he went up again to Independence to see Moore, and stayed with him all day; he returned towards night, and after supper went up and stayed with him all night, in the morning he returned and reported Mr. Moore on the gain — in the afternoon, Dr. Carr, one of our company, was going to Independence, and Dr. Palmer said he did not feel well, and wished him to call and see Moore. He did so, and on his return Sunday forenoon reported Moore a great deal better. About 4 o'clock on Saturday Dr. Palmer was called on to visit a patient about two miles from our camp; he went and saw the man, and returned in the evening. In the night he was sent for again to see the same man; he said he did not feel well, but wo'd go up in the morning. In the morning early he got up and went out, (he sleeps and messes with me,) returned in a few minutes and said he had the diarrhoea. I got up, and he asked me to tell Dr. Wells to get him some Rhubarb; Dr. Wells got the Rhubarb for him and he took it; he was told by some of the boys that he had better take some of his cholera medicine instead of physic, he said he wanted to physic, and then he would take the cholera medicine if it run him too hard; in the course of some three hours he had some four evacuations — his medicine did not operate, and then he commenced taking Opium and Camphor, and his prepared cholera medicine, but he had gone too far, he was so weak that he could not keep any medicines upon his stomach, but as often as taken was immediately thrown off by vomiting. I went after Dr. Carr, and he and Dr. Wells stayed with him until night. Injections were resorted to, and finally the evacuations were stopped, and at sundown he was considered a great deal better. He was rubbed constantly with brandy, hot drops and tinct. of lobelia, but his pulse was down and he could not be brought up. Dr. Wells and E.S. Camp stayed with him until 12 or 1 o'clock and worked faithful; at that time Dr. Carr was called, and Capt. Rawson, H. Camp, J.D. Potts, and others, stayed with him until he died. I was under a sweating operation, taken for a severe cold, and was sleeping in one of the wagons, and was not called until he was dead. He had the best of care and attention, and the best wishes of all his brethren in this expedition. No man stood higher in the affections of all the company than Dr. Palmer. His kind and affable manner endeared him to all, and I think I may safely say that no man in the company would be more sincerely mourned.

He was buried on the bluff about ¼ of a mile back from the Landing, known as the Blue Mill Landing, 6 miles below Independence; there is a small burying ground on the bluff where we buried him. I took a description of the ground, so that at any time his friends may find his grave; near the head of his grave, about 3 feet distant, stands a hickory, about 6 or 8 inches through, on which we marked the initials of his name, J.H.P. North-east some ten feet stands an elm, and 3 feet farther, in the same direction, stands a black walnut — directly north about 4 rods, stands an elm covered with Ivy — south 13 feet a black oak stub.

During the afternoon he said to Mr. E.S. Camp, (who was with him at the time,) here is my watch (handing it to him) which I wish you would take care of until I get well, but if I should not get well, give it to my sister. This was all he said on the subject of his death at any time.

Respectfully yours,
HORACE C. LADD

[May 30, 1849]   *INDEPENDENCE, May 16 – 12 M*

We arrived here this afternoon, and shall leave in about one hour. We broke up our camp yesterday, and came on our road some three miles – encamped for the night, and are now fairly on our way for the far west. My health is good, as well as that of most of the company. Some are a little unwell. One of our men is quite smart who had the cholera back at our old camp. We cured him with Palmer's medicine. Mr. Nichols, the Dagurreotype man, died the day after Dr. Palmer. No others have had cholera; and we think now that we shall escape any further attacks, as we take it by the forelock. The moment a man has symptoms of diarrhoea we give him a dose, and it has the desired effect. Nichols had had diarrhoea for a week before he was taken with the cholera; but would not take medicine until too late.

George Allcott and myself have charge of our wagon, and it would not do you good to see us driving oxen — or steers, for they are all young and unbroken; but they are learning fast. H.C.L.

BULL CREEK, 40 miles W. of Independence,

[June 13, 1849]   *May 20, 1849*

I am well and very rugged, my health was never better; all

the company are well with one exception, and he is on the mend. We are fairly out upon the plains; we have traveled two or part of two days upon them; there is plenty of water, but wood is very scarce, only very small patches of scrubby stuff around the springs; it is one vast sea of land, not much rolling but gently undulating; the feed is good; our cattle are doing well. This is Sunday, and we shall not move until about three o'clock, then about seven miles; we shall begin to go faster. I think we can average twenty miles per day; we shall go over quicker from appearances than mule teams; the companies that have them wish they had taken oxen; a company from New York is encamped with us; they are sorry they have mules, We have lost three of our company by Cholera, two before we started, the other last Friday; but we are now past its reach. It comes on universally with a diarrhoea, and there is no danger unless you suffer it to run. Those that had it were careless about it, but there is no one in camp now that is troubled with it. It should be checked and not allowed to run at all. Laudanum is good to do it with, but a stimulus should also be given if it commences violently.

Yours,   C.A.B.

[June 13, 1849]   *KAUKARUSHA RIVER, May 21, 1849.*

I have an opportunity to send a few words to you by a person going back; we are going along finely, and most all in good health, and those that have been in bad health are recovering fast; the air of the Plains is very bracing. As I wrote the other day, I never was in better health, tough as a bear; we shall ford this river this morning. I am the cook of our mess, and am exempt from driving oxen, and do not have to stand on guard only as a sergeant of the guard, four hours once in five nights. Potts is Captain; Mr. Hobart, Steward; we out travel most of the mule teams; this is, most of the way, the finest country I ever saw, the feed is great, and if we have no bad luck, we shall go it in fine style; we have the best out fit I have seen on the Plains, and the best lot of fellows.

CHARLES A. BARTON.

[June 27, 1849]   *THURSDAY, May 17, 1849*

We are now encamped for the night twenty miles on our way. To-day we have come twelve miles through a lovely prairie country. We crossed the Big Blue without much difficulty. The water was up to our wagon bottoms, that was all, so it was forded without loss to our provisions. The stream at the crossing was about twenty rods wide, with steep declivity at the aclivity or the margin. No accident save the breaking of a wagon tongue marred our journey. Although many of the cattle were unbroken and many drivers inexperienced, yet we were so fortunate as to proceed with regularity, and enough of dispatch for the beginning. After crossing the river, a piece of wood land extends for three miles before we reach again the open prairie. — On the way we overtook a train of Santa Fe wagons, heavily laden with goods. One of them had upset in a bad spot in the woods, and they were re-loading. I saw cases of clocks and looking glasses, &c. &c., strewed by the road side. The Santa Fe trade with the Missouri merchants is very extensive. They have large covered wagons capable of holding 6 or 7 ton, drawn by as many yoke of cattle. A Mr. Spencer, a young man formerly residing in Detroit, seeing the title of our company marked on our wagon covers, made some inquiries of me concerning Michigan. He is interested in the train above mentioned, and has been residing here for several years. — You would be surprised and delighted to see our camping ground this evening. Here on the verge, the limit of civilization, the most beautiful farms the eye ever saw.

It is about 10 o'clock A.M. We are still encamped on the edge of the timber on one side, and of the prairie on the other. Our blacksmith forge is erected, and Hoag and the other smiths are fastening chains to the wagons for locking the wheels. I hear from my tent the hammer sounding upon the anvil. It is a warm lovely day — the breeze on the prairie ground is cold and refreshing. Some of our men are cutting hickories to make some extra axles and tongues. The blankets and clothes are all spread out in the air. We lay by most of the day for these purposes. I have been down to a steam within a stone's throw, and enjoyed the luxury of a bath. All of my mess are out at work, heading our cattle where they are feeding finely, or at work otherwise, I am alone in the tent. Our cook, Mr. Fralick, is washing the clothes of our mess. Ours is called "the Star mess," and if good whole souled fellows who stand up to the work at all times, are entitled to that distinction, then our mess is not mis-named. Geo. Hoag works like a hero, he beats himself. I write on my trunk in a blank book, so that if an opportunity should occur to send you a letter, I can tear out what I have written and enclose to you in an envelope. From the door of my tent which faces the north, within thirty rods, across a beautiful stream, I can see a fine white farm house — the centre of one of the most splendid farms that can be cultivated on the face of the earth. In the rear of our tents are the wagons chained — the hind wheel of the one behind to the hind wheel of the one before, forming what is called a coral. In that space open at the ends we drove the cattle last night, and set watches upon them. I was on the 1st watch from 8 o'clock to ½ past 10 P.M. The watches were continued until ½ past 4 this morning, when the cattle were let out and herded. — This is a custom we shall keep up all the way through.

There are two wagons to each mess. Those *which* contain the *mess* chests last night were driven so as to form the lower line, and the other wagons the upper line of the coral. In this way the mess chests containing our dishes and rations, were all near our tents, which were pitched in a line north of the wagons, leaving space enough for cooking and eating between them. We have a nice out-fit. Each mess has a little stove and furniture, also table furniture, such as knives and forks, plates, spoons, basins, &c., plain but good — our plate is neither silver nor gold, but the real tin. We shall have to wait for gold plate until we return from California. After we are fairly started, we shall go ahead of any thing on the road, with our light wagons and young cattle. I think we shall get through here so as to move off 4 miles this afternoon. Herman Camp's voice I hear, he is hallowing at the top of his voice, "I tell you, every mess which wants its rations, to send along a man to get them, or I will shut up the bag."

Independence is the greatest little place for business that I ever saw. There is more gold and silver in circulation in and around it, than one sees (except in Banks) in large cities — it is a place upon which this year has rained plentifully a golden harvest.

May 20, 1849.
Bull Creek, 45 miles from Independence.

We reached this spot last evening when the sun was about ½ an hour high. Friday afternoon we struck our tents and traveled about 9 miles, which took us until sometime after dark. One mess wagon lingered behind containing in one of the wagons a member sick of the Cholera. It was Mr. Ives, a very worthy member. He died about 5 A.M. Saturday morning and was buried, and the mess came on and joined the train. Yesterday another, Mr. Highly, was severely attacked. He rode on with the train, and when we encamped last night he was carefully and faithfully attended to all night by his mess, and this morning we were gladdened to learn that he was better.

The fearful scourge seems to have become seated in our midst. Many are complaining, indeed but few who have not experienced symptoms calculated to excite apprehension and alarm. Where it is to end, God only knows. — I hope and pray that the cup may pass from us without having to drink of it deeper. May God in his providential dealings with us, spare, if consistent with His high and holy purposes. We are encamped near Bull Creek, a fine stream where ourselves and stock can rest and refresh. Near us is Capt. McNulty's company from New York — he has had several cases of the Cholera among his men, but his practice has been blessed and he has met with no loss of men. He goes with wagons and mules, and I presume will be near us often on the way. We are traveling through a country which for its vastness and beauty calls for exclamations of astonishment and delight. A hard, excellent, smooth and well defined road lies across prairies boundless in their range. As the train moves slowly along, the scene is picturesque in the highest degree. We are scarcely out of sight of emigrants at any time, although the throng is in advance. We stopped to rest at noon yesterday at the 'lone elm,' which stands one of nature's land marks in these vast solitudes. It is the only tree within a vast distance standing in a muddy stream, and is fast being hacked away by the travelers for fire wood. There seems no vestige of life remaining to it, but there it stands in its naked, withered loneliness. Mrs. Sigourney would find in it a fine subject for a beautiful subject.

Here at Bull Creek is an Indian hut with an enclosure of few acres of land, left desolate. — An old Indian was the inhabitant, but left it to-day for the 'West,' to escape the tide of population and the dread scourge attending it. How can the poor Indian escape! Where can he go? Here the Santa Fe road and the one usually traveled by the California emigrants, separate. We diverged from the latter road about a quarter of a mile from the lake of this camping ground. When we move again we shall leave the Santa Fe road to our left. The Ithaca company went along here the other day we learn. They take the Santa Fe road and expect to go by Bent's Fort, skipping along where wagon trains are impracticable. They were all well. Dr. Ormsby and the company of which he is a member are encamped on the creek near us. Our crowd is so large that we seem like a village whenever we stop. All compliment us as the finest crowd in our out-fit and appearance on the road. We are joined to-day by Mr. Smith, a young man from Battle Creek, with two companions — they are to travel under our regulations but their own wagon and outfit. Mr. Moore, who originally started with him from B. Creek, has been sick for week or two with the Cholera, and it has at length terminated fatally.

In Camp, May 25th.

The sun shines brightly after one of the most terrible storms of thunder, wind and rain, during the whole of last night and the most of yesterday afternoon. Night before last we encamped on the Wahanissi Creek, 60 miles on our way — the stream is a narrow, rapid current, with high banks forded with much labor. An Indian of the Shawnee nation has a house and an enclosure at the bank, and makes money by the handsfull out of the emigrants. He is a shrewd, agreeable man and understands well how to trade. Wanting to purchase a few more ponies, Mr. Ladd, four others and myself, started with the Indian leaving our train to pass on. We were on foot and travelled to the Kansas river which divides the Shawnees from the Delawares, crossed the river in a canoe and landed on the side of the Delawares. The river is wide and muddy having high banks where we crossed. On we went until we arrived at an Indian habitation. The Indians are settled near each other in the woodlands which abounds in these prairies, much after the manner of the Whites in Missouri. Their houses exhibit much taste in their construction, and the two tribes — the Delawares and the Shawnees are quite advanced in the art of agriculture. They have fine stock and appear to live much at their ease. We were armed to the teeth, but on account of the consternation which prevails among the Indians on account of the Cholera, we could hardly get sight of them. They avoided us and dare not let us into their houses, or approach too near themselves – until they hurried away from us as if death attended our steps – our arms were useless, for we carried with us in their imagination, a protection more formidable, in the fear of the dread scourge which has spread among them. Only three of them dared to approach us, (although they have an abundance of horses for sale,) mounted each on a pony which we bought and which were all we could purchase of them. At 5 o'clock P.M. we re-crossed the river on our return arrived at the Wahanissi Creek the place we set out from in the morning, at 6 P.M., having sent the Indian who acted as our guide, ahead to prepare supper for us. It really was a luxury for us to get under the roof of a log house where was a good fire, and see the supper preparing – we were wet, tired and hungry, but in good spirits. The hut was well made with glass windows and panes, doors, &c., and was well furnished with tables, chairs, cooking utensils, dishes &c. The Indian has some supplies such as Sugar, Coffee, &c., which he sells, and prepares meals for those who want them. He cooked us some bacon, baked two fine corn cakes in a bake kettle, gave us a cup of coffee and plenty of milk. Refreshed by our meal, we started to overtake our train. We crossed the creek, passed thro' a mile of woods, thence into a wide strip of marshy lowland – saw all along companies laboring to drive on their mules, and others already encamped for the night. Then our road became harder, the rain nevertheless, pouring down in torrents as onward we pushed our way – now the darkness and the storm increased, save by the glare of the lightning we could see nothing – on, on, we moved, slowly, expecting every moment to see a light and at last we supposed we would have to spend the night in the rain on the prairies. A while afterwards we saw a light which shone like a lone-star in the heavens. By the lightning we saw the white covers glitter in the distance, we set up a shout and moved faster up a hill to where we supposed we would find our camp. On approaching the spot — "who goes there?" sounded in our ears, and we found it to be the camp of a Virginia company. They informed us that our company was about a mile ahead, over a very high and difficult hill. On we trudged and after going about three miles further and slipping down several times in the mud, we arrived at our camp. We were all soaking wet, it was about eleven o'clock. Soon after I got to bed and asleep, the storm which had been increasing in fury all the while, shook our tents so that the pins would not hold it. We arose, struck our tents and retreated to the wagons. I lay my head forward on a barrel and was seated on a large bellows, and that was my luxurious bed. To-day all is right again, I have heard of no one taking cold from the exposure of the night — what is still better, I think we shall have no more trouble from the cholera, the hand of death has been stayed, the men are recovering their good spirits.

Oh that I had time and talent to describe the glorious country through which we are passing; every day's travel opens new beauties and unfolds new scenes to admire. We are now on a high hill from which all varieties of prairie scenes appear; about a mile south of the camp lies a descending green which sparkles in its freshness.

Indian Town, May 28.

Arrived here to-day, 110 miles from Independence. The weather is fine, the roads good, the health of the company neatly restored.

This is quite a settlement. There are seven stores — all kinds of goods suitable for emigrants; White men own them. This village looks like civilization, the houses and stores are of logs, rudely, but well constructed; about 80 houses here.

We shall try to cross the Kansas river at the ferry this afternoon. Mr. Potts is our Captain and things move briskly. We
lost a man named Lyon this morning who has not been well
for some time but imprudently declined doing anything for
himself.

May 29th.

We are still at the ferry. One of the boats sprung a leak
and sank, which had delayed wagons in advance of us, there
is now but one boat.

There are many things in our camp life agreeable as well
as some that are tough. We work hard, eat largely, sleep sound-
ly, and those of us who are well, enjoy it vastly. We have not
when traveling averaged over 10 miles a day, but one day we
went 23 miles. Many of our company have purchased mules.
We shall soon begin to travel faster, we can average 20 miles
a day, or make 120 miles a week, which will soon bring us into
the pictures. I hear Capt. Potts ordering our wagons moved
down to the river's brink so as to occupy the ground next to the
ferry and thus prevent back teams getting ahead of us, I have
no right while preparation is being made to cross the river, to
enjoy myself in communion with home.

[July 4, 1849]   *Kansas' Ferry, May 28, 1849.*

FRIEND LEWIS: — At length we have come after much
of labor to this spot, one of the landmarks on the route, to de-
note progress, and the very last from which frequent communication is had with the States. We have met on our way,
many moving as we have moved. We have seen some returning who lacked the fortitude and perseverance to proceed. We
have seen some perilous times, when it seemed as if the hand
of the Almighty had marked us for destruction, through the

agency of that scourge whose appearance this spring was prognosticated, and whose march has prostrated four of our party, cutting short their journey in life, and thereby extinguishing the star of hope that guided them to undertake their long and perilous trip. They have gone — we mourn their loss, but do not despond. The same arm that has preserved us thus far, in scenes calculated to make the stoutest heart falter, and the face of the strongest to blanch, can safely protect in dangers as yet unseen. The spirits of our party, in spite of the appalling events alluded to, continue elastic and buoyant, and the world is onward to the end.

Our teams are waiting at the river's brink, for some 30 wagons in advance of us to cross, before our turn comes. In all probability we shall get across this afternoon as the river is not wide, and two boats are constantly employed carrying over two wagons each, at once. Our oxen we shall swim over. The banks of the river are high, but there is a good ingress and egress. A beautiful strip of timber adorns the banks on both sides. I write upon the ground, beneath the shade of a large oak, which for years has afforded shade to the Indian in these solitudes, now disturbed by the resistless tide of emigration rolling westward. This is the land of the Pottawatomies, and some of our company have found those they were acquainted with in Michigan, among the little troops of Indians well mounted who have rode along by our side for a day or two past. Their land was purchased of the Kansas or Caw Indians, as they are called, by the Government, and the Pottawatomies who were divided and scattered, were brought together and located here. They seem to live much at their ease. Gaily dressed, with flowing robes and the shining turbans, mounted on ponies dashingly caprisoned, they gallop up apparently proud and happy. Yet some are returning to their old home; for they say the hunt is not good here, and their recollections doubtless endear them to the lands of their fathers. Their territory on this side the river runs east to the

Wahanissie Creek when the Shawnees' begins. There are quite a number of whites living with the Indians. About a mile from this ferry is what is called Indian Town, quite a large village containing 9 stores kept by Traders. Many goods are sold there this year to the emigrants, and always to the Indians. The latter are soon to receive another payment, and the Traders are ready for the harvest. They are not allowed to sell liquor to the Indians, who have frequently made applications to us for the article, but in vain. It is thought that this land of the Shawnees and Pottawatomies, will soon be in market. It seems to me it is inevitable that it must be cultivated. It is a country which surpasses any thing I ever saw for beauty, and for agricultural purposes. It is well wooded and watered, and the rich soil invites the labor of the husbandman. Some of the Indians do a little at farming; but they never will develop the resources of a great State that might lie directly west of the Missouri. This California movement if it does nothing else, cannot fail to open the eyes of the people to the vastness and richness of the land over which we move, and cannot fail to bring about a re-consideration of that policy of the Government which restrains the white man from occupying and cultivating it. Gladly dear sir, would I describe to you the country with more particularity through which we are passing, had I the time, or the power to do it justice. It requires the painter's easel, or the poet's inspiration, to communicate to one unseeing, a proper conception of its thousand charms. Holding neither the pencil, nor engifted in song I can only say *"this is great country.!"*

I have seen some of the Shawnees, the Delawares who are across the river below, and the present nation, and they are peaceable, innoffensive people, fond of ease and display. If they could live with the whites without imbibing their vices, they might become good citizens. The Indian in the course of years, has either to become exterminated, or else he is to be taught to cultivate the soil, read and write, to pursue industrious and laborious occupations — let men think of this, and let such a course be taken with them as will gradually elevate them in the scale of being, and show to them that they, as well as we, have in interest in this government of ours, more valuable than any thing they have lost in the history of the past.

We shall soon be among the Pawnees, and as we travel on, the red man in his wilderness will appear. Stories have been circulated here and elsewhere, that Emigrants have been attacked, plundered and slaughtered, this Spring — but it is not so; for some have returned since the events imagined, were said to have taken place, who declare it false; yet the stories have alarmed some timid men to retrace their steps. The best intelligence from the plains, is, that emigration moves on safely, not only from the Indians, but also that Cholera has left the track.

I have not time to add more now. Wishing you continued health and prosperity, I remain yours truly,   J.P.

CAMP WOL. RANGERS, near Little Blue River,
[July 11, 1849]   *June 7, 1849 — 12 M.*

Shortly after writing my last letter, which was dated at Kansas Ferry, I was taken with the billious diarrhoea, and had a hard time of it for two days, but was not so bad but what I kept on with the train. I have never felt better than I do now. Our whole company is well, with but one man who is not able to do camp duty. We are all cheerful and happy, and but for the deprivation of the society of our families, never enjoyed ourselves better. We are entirely beyond the influence of cholera, and are traveling through one of the most beautiful countries eye ever rested upon. We have drove about 11 miles this morning, and are now enjoying our noon rest.

Our hour of rising in the morning is 4 o'clock — hitch up and start at half past 6 — drive until 11 — rest until 2 — and drive until 6 in the evening. The roads now are first rate, and we are making from 17 to 20 miles per day. We have been driving slow heretofore, in order to recruit our cattle; they are now in fine order, and we begin to push ahead.

We have not seen an Indian since crossing the Kansas Ferry, and shall not until we reach Fort Kearney. The Pawnees (in whose country we are now traveling) and the Sioux have been at war all the spring, and the U.S. officers have interfered, and a council of the two nations is called at Fort Kearney on the 10th of this month. The Fort is about 100 miles from here, and we shall probably be there before the Indians leave, and will have a chance to see some of the tribes.

We have heard all sorts of stories about sickness, cholera, small pox, and Indians, on our road; but they are all false as can be, and you must not believe any of them. We saw an officer from Fort Kearney this morning, and he tells us there is no sickness ahead, and that those stories are got up to scare some emigrants going west. We meet once in a while some of the Californians who are returning. They have seen the tail of the elephant, and can't bear to look any farther. Poor forsaken looking beings they are, I assure you. Some are on foot, and some on horseback, and we see now and then one with wagon and oxen. But our motto is go ahead! I don't think there is a man in our company to-day who would sell his interest for $500.

Last night there came up about five o'clock one of the most violent thunder storms I ever saw. Our coral ring was immediately formed, tents pitched, and ditched all around; and we sat during the storm in our tents cooking our supper and cracking our jokes, dryer and more comfortable than we would have been in a great many of our houses in Marshall. In fact, we have not been either wet or cold but once since we left, and that scene was described in my last letter.

We have plenty of provisions, and they are well cooked. By the way, I am cook, and Geo. Alcott is assistant cook. ****** But "Oh; cracky!" if you could see what a black looking set of boys we are, you would think, if we were not Indians, we had certainly been where they were. The teams are hitching up, and I must close for the present. I will write again from Fort Kearney, if I have a chance.

Yours in haste,   HORACE.

Camp Wolverine Rangers — Little Blue,

[July 18, 1849]   June 10, 1849.

DEAR SIR: — I embrace the opportunity afforded by the arrival of a train of traders bound to the States with Buffalo Hides to write a line or two of our whereabouts and of our condition. We are encamped to-day (Sunday) on a small stream of good water a tributary of the Little Blue, which we reached last evening about sun-set, after a Saturdays journey of 27 miles. Glad were we when from the Prairie upon which we had diverged for the Little Blue the stream appeared. For several days past the water has been disagreeable to the taste, and not very plentiful at that, except as found in the river along which with an occasional divergence we are traveling. Indeed the water of the Little Blue is far from being as palatable as that to which we have been used. Covered with dust — the men and teams thirsty and fatigued — the common blessings of wood and water were realized, and when the stream skirted with timber hove in sight a thrill of delight passed along the train and the drivers gave an extra crack to their whips eager for supper and rest.

Several smaller companies are traveling in our train, and carolling with our company; we frequently pass other companies of emigrants, and for the last week scarce a day has elapsed without meeting Emigrants or others returning from a nearer view of the Elephant than we have yet enjoyed.

I have not time now, for tent duties occupy me, to enter at all into a description of the Country through which we are now journeying. We are now 40 miles from the Platte — and 60 from Fort Kearney. We learn that the Pawnees in whose country we now are (but none of whom we have yet seen) and the Sioux who have been at war with each other meet to day at the Fort under the auspices and by the efforts of Government officers there to make a treaty of peace. We hope they will continue together at least two or three days, so that we may have a look at them in Council assembled. Our Company are in good health and are all ready for what is ahead.

I will write from Fort Kearney if possible as I am at this moment much hurried, Yours, &c.

J.P.

In addition to the above letter we have been permitted to make the following extracts from a letter of the same date from H.C. Ladd to his father, which contains many items of interest not before published:

'Grass is abundant, and our cattle are getting as fat as pigs, though we have commenced pushing ahead. We drove last week, in six days 118 miles, to-morrow we calculate on traveling 20 miles, when we shall camp for the night and take in wood and water for next day's march, which will be 25 miles, to the Platte River, without wood or water; but we can go it. We came 27 yesterday. We have a man with us from St. Louis who has a Miledrometer which tells us every night how far we have traveled. We are on the same trail that Bryant traveled in 1846, and have gained seven days of him from Independence here, and are confident that we are doing well.

We calculate on being at the South Pass in 6 weeks at

fartherest. There are a great many on the road, and we see trains every day. We passed one of 26 wagons last night that crossed the Kansas two days ahead of us. We have passed two mule trains, and are confident that with our light wagons we can pass a great many this side of the Mountains. Our wagons have proved to be first rate; and such roads as we are traveling now you never saw — they are as smooth as Main St. in Marshall.

Our company are all well, except Van Brunt, from Dry Prairie; he had the chill fever, and has not got strong yet. We have several other wagons traveling with us, three from Plymouth and one from Ypsilanti, belonging to Mr. Graham, whose teamster today met with a sad accident. He had set his gun up against the side of the wagon, and while throwing out some bedding the bundle struck the gun and it went off, and the charge went into his leg just below the knee, breaking his leg and injuring the knee. We shall probable leave him at Fort Kearney (60 miles from here) under the charge of the Surgeon.

A man who has charge of a train of wagons, loaded with Buffalo robes, and who has just came from Fort Laramie, says there is no sickness west of us. Tom Manser is in first rate spirits and stands the jaunt good: We had a good time combing each others heads and shaving this morning — after which we went down to the river and washed our shirts, stockings, pants and towels, and then went a fishing till night — but caught fisherman's luck only.

Mr. Rawson is cook of our mess now. We had for tea good light biscuit, dried apple sauce, goosebury's stewed, hard bread, tea and dried beef — so you see we are not starving in this prairie land. I went out hunting with three others yesterday, but got nothing. We saw 3 hares, 3 antelope, and a large grey wolf; but they were all off before we came near enough to give them a shot.

We met a fur trader a few days since, from the west, who

brought great news from the gold diggings. I shall write again soon.

NEW FORT KEARNEY, PLATTE RIVER VALLEY,
[August 15, 1849]   *June 13, 1849*

DEAR SIR: — When I left home I supposed there would be much leisure time to devote to writing. But such is not the fact on this route. In the morning from day-light to the moment of starting which is usually 6 o'clock A.M. our whole time is employed in duties indispensable to this roving camp life of ours – when we halt for an hour and a half at noon, dinner has to be prepared and rest taken for the afternoons work. When we encamp at night supper is the first matter of interest to be attended to — then the tent to be pitched — the trench to be digged —and then tired nature seeks the sweet restorer, balmy sleep. Even then are we fortunate if the Morning Star finds us sleeping or in repose, for frequently it happens that we have to seek refuge from our beds to our India Rubbers to protect from the pelting storms; for terrific thunder showers accompanied by high winds before which tents shake and fall are not unusual to the country. We are still in the territory of the Pawnees, yet have seen no specimen of that thieving mischievous tribe. We heard the other day that a large party of the Cheyennes were on the war path, molesting small trains of emigrants, but none of them ever have crossed our path or darkened by their grim shadows our career. The rumor that a treaty was in contemplation between the Sioux and Pawnees to come off soon at the fort turns out to be merely a fable. We now learn that the Sioux decline any compromise with their ancient enemies. We are now encamped within four miles of New Fort Kearney which is situated in the valley of the Platte, about a mile from the river near Grand Island. The fort and other buildings show evidences of newness, being built of prairie sods, the soldiers and officers living in tents. There are about 150 soldiers in the garrison, and several disabled and sick emigrants in the Hospital. A small party left our camp a day or two since with a young man who was wounded by the accidental discharge of his gun to get admittance for him at the fort; we learn to day that they have not yet succeeded though a prospect is held out that he may be admitted. He has however the attendance of Government surgeons. He is a young man of the name of McKinney, a resident of Maine who was one of a Plymouth company which travels and carols with us, for mutual protection. His wound is a bad one in the knee made with buck-shot, which will probably cripple him for life, preventing him from prosecuting his trip with his company.

The valley of the Platte where we now are is about three miles wide — on one side bounded by a range of bluffs — on the other by a tract of timber skirting the shore. The river is not in sight here. We were informed by a white settler here to day that this was once one of the best ranges for the Buffalo in the world. And yet we have seen none of that game. The other day in the valley of the Little Blue several elk, very wild were seen and one of our company Mr. Seymour was fortunate enough to shoot and bring one into camp creating quite a sensation. The next day each of the messes had a sufficiency to make a stew-pie of the portions which relished well, I assure you, to those who had regaled themselves on no other meat than bacon for a month. We have now accomplished 320 miles of our journey in a period of four weeks to day from the time we left Independence. It is always considered good time to make the Platte in a month from that point. Our teams are in a flourishing condition and we are averaging 20 miles per day. The health of our company is completely restored, and all things move off briskly. It is 320 miles to Ft. Laramie from here, which we expect to reach by the 4th of July, and where we shall if no unforseen accident occurs celebrate the anniversary of our National Independence. We learn that there are two stores there, but if things are as dear as at Fort Kearney our goods will not be increased much at that point. A few days since we met some emigrants returning and bought 70 lbs. Coffee on the plains at 7 cents per lb. The rest of their traps they had disposed of. Every day we meet some one, traders, emigrants or others returning to the States. Day before yesterday a small escort of dragoons accompanying Maj. Belger to the frontier from this fort. There are 10 or 12 companies of emigrants in our vicinity whom we have overtaken. The great mass is far ahead, some as far as the South Pass.

It is late and I am wearied — you will please excuse this hasty written letter. Yours, J.P.

P.S. Thursday noon — June 14th.

Train at the fort. — Many things we find can be bought here after all reasonably. There is one store full of goods. The turf fortifications look snug and comfortable and seem strong enough backed by American regulars with their field pieces and muskets for the occasion. We stop here an hour then take up our march. Yours, J.P.

[September 12, 1849] *[From the Sheboygan Mercury]*

In Camp on the Banks of the Platte 50 miles west of Fort Laramie, July 8, '49.

DEAR BROTHER: — I have an opportunity of sending a letter to the States by a gentleman who is on his return home. It is no uncommon occurrence for us to meet return parties, who have become discouraged, home-sick and affrighted at the difficulties in the way and who have turned their backs upon the enterprise, even after having accomplished more than two-thirds of the journey from their homes.

Every return party we have met, has told of us of the difficulties just ahead, and could you see their long and doleful faces you would think them almost insurmountable, but we have found them comparatively easy to overcome. We have been steadily moving on and meeting with eminent success. We have found ourselves thus far equal to the enterprise, and we expect to be equal to cope with any hazard or difficulty that may present itself even to our journey's end. We are now 730 miles from Independence, and about 200 miles from the south pass in the Rocky mountains which we expect to reach by the first of August. We are now moving at the rate of 110 miles per week.

The amount of suffering endured, and the sacrifice of property by those who have preceded us, is truly appalling. That dread scourge, the cholera, has run through the whole line. Hundreds that have left their homes with the brightest anticipations are now mouldering upon the plains. Were there no other marks, to guide the emigrant upon his way, the graves upon either side of the trail would be sufficient to direct him with unerring certainty for hundreds of miles. We have frequently passed from 8 to 15 graves in a single day's drive. Almost every State in the Union has been called upon to mourn the loss of a portion of their emigrant companies; but in this respect, the South has been the most afflicted. The companies from the northern States, seem to endure the hardships and stand the change of climate much the best.

In regard to the destruction and desertion of property, you would scarcely believe the account. Cattle that have become sore footed or fagged out are roaming all over the plains. The road on either side for the last hundred miles has been literally strewn with broken waggons and even those that were sound and good: with stoves, trunks, cooking utensils, Iron, steel, barrels, boxes, black smith tools of almost all kinds, broken chains and provisions. Yesterday we passed several piles of most beautiful bacon, which had been thrown away

[47]

by companies preceding us, to lighten their loads. If any of the companies fail of reaching their destination it will be those who have thrown away their provisions to make greater speed. They have become foolishly alarmed, and are now rushing ahead like mad men. Their cattle are fast failing, and I fear the result will be, that their teams will entirely fail before they pass the mountains and they will be left destitute of provisions.

I should be glad to give you a description of the country through which we have passed and a few incidents of our journey. Some of them I know would be exceedingly interesting, but I must forbear at present, not having leisure time to do so. Suffice it to say, that parts of the country cannot be exceeded in beauty of scenery, while other parts are void of interest. There is sufficient however to make it extremely interesting to the traveler, and sufficiently dangerous to try the stuff of which he is made. As for myself, the journey has been one of peculiar interest. I have enjoyed excellent health during the whole time, and have been at all times able to enter into the sports incident to our journey. I have chased the huge Buffalo for eight miles over his native plains, under whip and spur, with a recklessness that would astonish you, frequently scaling the highest bluffs and leaping into the low ravines where it appeared impossible for a horse to go. I have chased the antelope and wolf in droves. I have murdered whole nests of the most enormous rattle snakes. — I have tried the mettle of my revolver in shooting the prairie dog. I have seen the hail stones fall that would weigh 1½ pounds cutting the heads of our men in gashes and making seives of our waggon covers. I have witnessed and been engaged in many other scenes the most exciting as well as interesting, and of which you will be fully informed when you receive my journal.

ELMON S. CAMP.

IN CAMP, 50 MILES WEST OF FT. LARAMIE,

[September 5, 1849]   July 8, 1849

DEAR MARY EDNA, AND OTHERS: — Last evening a man by the name of ———————— came into our camp and remained with us during the night. His teams are back some four or five miles, and as soon as they arrive he is going on to Independence. He has become disheartened, and lost all ambition. He thinks he has seen the elephant, and has had enough of going to California. While he is waiting for his teams to come up, I shall continue writing, and forward my letter to the States. I wrote you when at Kearney, some 350 miles east of this. Since we left the Kansas river, some 625 miles back there has been no sickness in our camp. Our men have all been rugged and hearty, and are constantly becoming more so every day.

Every thing moves on prosperously thus far. We are now 730 miles from Independence, and 1930 miles from Marshall. We were 3 weeks in coming from Ft. Kearney to Ft. Laramie, a distance of 300 miles. We travel about 100 miles per week, (we have for 6 weeks past.) The country around us and along the line of our march presents to the eye the most sublime and picturesque appearance. Often we see a distance of 100 to 200 miles, over rolling prairies and along high mountain ranges. For 8 days we have been in sight of Laramie's Peak, during which time we have been traveling towards it, and are now at least 50 miles from it.

While passing through the buffalo country east of Ft. Laramie our men had fine sport in the chase. I will give you a full description of our day's movements, that you may be able to judge more fully some of the thrilling events we witness. At 4 o'clock in the morning of the 20th of June, at the sound of the bugle, the company were aroused to commence the labors of the day, (we are very early risers this trip.) The cattle having been turned out of coral to feed, the herdsmen might be seen off on the plain keeping them from scattering, and in readiness to drive them in at the sound of the bugle. As soon after the men were up as possible you might see the smoke curling up from a dozen stoves, and every preparation in the culinary department being made by the cooks, while others were greasing the wagons for the day's march. At 5 o'clock breakfast. At half past the horn blows for the cattle to be driven into coral and yoked up and hitched to the wagons. At 6 o'clock the whole train is in motion. Early in the morning we discovered that five of our horses were missing, which we discovered, by using our telescope, some eight miles distant, making their way back towards the States. Three of our men on horseback were sent in pursuit of them, (E.S. Camp, H.C. Ladd, and Mr. Root.) Before they returned, the train had advanced some two miles. While they were returning, they started a large herd of buffaloes, and drove them between our train and the river Platte, which was some 2½ or 3 miles from us. A large party of men having turned off from the road to go to the river a little in advance of the train, discovered the buffalo ahead, and turned them directly towards our train. Our hunters, and in fact almost every man, had his gun in readiness to give them a hearty welcome as soon as they came within shooting distance; while others on foot and on horseback ran to meet them as they made their way towards the bluffs, some two miles distant, on the appearance of our train. As they broke through our train, a general rush was made upon them. In a moment all was excitement and confusion. The shooting of the guns — the shouts of the men — the snuffing and bellowing of the frightened and wounded animals — the barking and yelping of the dogs – and the whipping and slashing, as well as scolding and yelling, of the teamsters, to keep the frightened cattle from breaking loose from the train — all tended to one general scene of consternation and confusion; whilst it constituted a sight the most exalting, as well as the most pleasing and exciting, I ever expected to enjoy. A large number of the animals were wounded at the first volley, and lagged behind the herd as they were rushing over the plain and straining every nerve to gain the heights. It was but the work of a moment for our men to reload and make a second charge upon the wounded animals, three of which lay struggling in the agonies of death before they had advanced far from the train. The fourth and fifth were soon after brought to the ground by those who continued the chase. A description of such a scene is impossible, is beyond my ability to portray. The grandeur of the scenery upon the stage that this scene was enacted, was alone calculated to produce feelings of grandeur as the eye was filled with the wild beauty of extended prairie, with mountain bluffs on one side and the majestic Platte rolling its waters eastward on the other. Our train stopped long enough to take on some of the choicest pieces of the meat, after the game had been dressed. At 12 o'clock we halted for nooning, the cattle turned out to feed, and dinner prepared. All were delighted with the sports of the day, as well as the pleasure in partaking of the luxury of the meat prepared by our most experienced cooks. At half past 1 o'clock our train was again in motion. You cannot imagine the stream of pleasure that ran through every mind as we proceeded on our way, talking over the part each acted in the drama of the past. At half past 2 o'clock the clouds began to thicken in the northwest, threatening us with a heavy shower. Soon peal after peal of thunder seemed to roll around the plain, while the forked lightning was constantly darting across the thick gathering blackness — dense clouds which were fast approaching; and soon to our great surprise, we heard a deep heavy roaring sound in the direction of the storm. In a few moments after large hail stones commenced dropping in every direction around us. I was on my horse a few rods in advance of the train; I immediately turned about and rode along down the train, telling the teamsters to take their oxen off the wagons. Before I had got half way down the train, the storm burst upon us in all its fury. In a moment all was wild confusion; a torrent of hail stones was pouring down upon us from the size of hen's eggs to at least the size of goose eggs; teamsters could not manage their teams; the teams immediately whirled round and ran with the storm, some with and some without the wagons being attached to them; some of the wagons were upset by the teams turning too short; wagon tongues were broken off; some of our men got under the wagons that were free from the teams; some got into the wagons that the teams were running with; some jumped from their horses and got under the first wagon stationary they could reach. While many were thus doing they were knocked down by the hail; many had large holes cut in their heads; others were wounded on their arms, hands, shoulders and backs. The storm lasted about 12 to 15 minutes. As soon as it was over, you might see at least 20 men, some with blood streaming down their faces; others with their hands covered with blood, all in search of the Doctor to get their wounds dressed and attended to; while others were some miles distant on the plain in pursuit of their teams, some of which had run over a mile and a half. All looked like a perfect shipwreck, and for a few minutes during the heaviest of the storm, I thought our whole expedition would be broken up, and we be obliged to give up the enterprise. Wm. Williams, Lewis Winchester, Wm. Delong, Capt. Thomas Rawson, and myself, went in pursuit of the horses, which had also run with the storm. We found them some 3½ miles from the train, with their saddles and bridles on, all sound. They were near our nooning place. After we had proceeded some two miles from the wagons, we noticed that the hail stones were very much larger than we had before seen, and near the ground where we nooned the hail stones were at least six inches deep on the ground, and many of them that were from 4 to 5 inches in diameter; and it was the opinion of all of us present that some of the largest ones would weigh a pound and a half, and if melted would make a pint and a half of water. I could not help feeling thankful that we were not on our nooning ground during the storm. I am certain if we had been we would have lost many of our cattle, and no doubt some of our men. When we returned to the train we found all the men at work repairing the damages, and making preparations to start again. In about two hours the train was again moving. Some of the wounded were in wagons, and others with their heads bandaged and their arms suspended in slings, were walking by the side of the teams, narrating the part they severally acted in the last drama. I would that I could give any thing like a description of the feelings and appearance of each and every witness of this day's wonders. The clouds passed away, the sun set clear in the west, and all was tranquil.

We encamp on the valley of the Platte for the night at 6 ½ o'clock. The balance of the day was spent in the usual routine of duties, such as forming a carol of our wagons to shut up our cattle, in herding the cattle, cooking suppers, washing dishes, pitching tents, &c.; which usually takes us till about half past 8 o'clock. Thus you see that from 4 o'clock in the morning till about 9 in the evening, we are kept busy.

We are now about 200 miles from the South Pass of the Rocky Mountains, and if our usual success attends us we shall be there before the 25th inst. On the 30th of June, H.C. Ladd was thrown from his horse, or, in other words, a wounded buffalo bull, mad and furious, in consequence of being wounded, made a charge upon his horse. The horse, also being intoxicated with the sport, would not mind the spur or bit; but seemed determined to rush upon the wounded animal, the result of which was that the buffalo caught the horse in the flank and threw him some 20 feet, and his rider nearly as much farther. Fortunately, however, Mr. Ladd sustained no personal injury, save being very much frightened, from which

[53]

he has fully recovered. The horse was badly wounded and bled very profusely. He is fast recovering.

We halted at or near the remains of Ft. Bernard, some 7 or 8 miles East of Fort Laramie on the evening of the 3d of July, to prepare to spend the 4th. We celebrated the day with as much patriotism as we could have in the States. At sunrise a salute of 13 guns was fired. The committees commenced performing their several duties. The wagons were hauled in two rows about 15 feet apart, and their covers stretched across to form an awning — under which a table was set 100 feet long, and also with seats for 100 men, that being the number in our train — at 11½ Prayer, by Rev. Mr. Hobart; Reading Declaration of Independence, by James Pratt; Oration, by Mr. Sexton, (a student of Ann Arbor University), during which, at proper periods, music. After which a procession was formed and we marched to the banquet of fat and luxurious things which covered our board. There were among the items thus placed before us — Boiled ham, excellent; boiled and baked beans, buffalo meat cooked in different ways, good bread and biscuit, fried cakes sweetened and unsweetened, various kinds of baked cakes, and ginger-bread, apple pies, peach pies and plumb pies, assorted pickles put up in jars, corn bread, johnny cake, dried beef, buffalo meat, apple sauce, peach sauce and plumb sauce, rice and bread and Indian puddings, good coffee, lemonade and spirits — all of which were greedily partaken of. The above sketch will give you some idea how we poor fellows do suffer out here on the plains. After the dinner was over, the regular toasts of the day were read by Mr. Pratt, after which volunteer toasts were given by most all the men present. If there were time and room I would give some of the toasts.

I stopped a short time at Fort Laramie, and was informed by Major Sanderson that he, as the agent of the government, had purchased the Fort of the American Fur Company for the sum of $4,000. There is one company of troops there, and two more companies expected to arrive soon. They have about 100 men now engaged in getting out timber and materials for a new fort of barracks. They are building a saw mill and design to have it running time enough to make lumber with this season. There is plenty of pine timber within 10 or 12 miles of the Fort.

We have seen but 5 Indians since we left the Kansas River. It is no uncommon thing to meet returning parties on their way back to the States, who have become disheartened and discouraged. We look upon such as wanting in that element that can alone prepare men to meet and surmount the hardships of a trip like this. Such men ought never to have started. Some imagine they see the Elephant before they witness any hardships at all. The teams of our guest have arrived, and he is now waiting for me to fold up my letter.

In haste,   H.CAMP

We are particularly requested to publish the following letter, which was a sort of P.S. to the above:

To my Dear Molly: — I wrote to you from Ft. Laramie. I should write to you again now, had I time; but I am drafted upon the committee to cut hay to-day and cannot. Herman is writing a general letter to all, which will give you a history of all our doings, and he says he will direct it so that you can see it. Give my respects to mother P. and all others.

Yours, &c.   E.S. CAMP

Extracts from a letter to Mrs. Barton, of the same date as the above: "We are now making hay to take with us to the ferry of the Platte, as we have two days travel without much feed. There we shall feed our cattle a couple of days, cut hay enough to last four days more. We have 2,000 lbs. of corn and 3,000 lbs. of meal which we can give our cattle if necessary. Our only trouble is feed for our cattle. The road is good; none better in the States. There is one thing certain, every one that sees our wagons allows if any train on this road can go over the plains the Rangers can do it. Our light wagons, light loads and strong teams are not equaled on this route. Our men are all well and hearty, and the go-ahead is in them. The Pioneer Line of stages is only five days ahead, and we have left a good many mule trains behind us. There is a train about two miles ahead, that is half women; a great many of them have gone over, and we have seen but three graves. They stand it better than the average of men. The troops have more than half of them deserted. A good many of the trains talk of going to Oregon to stay through the winter. I hope they will, for we are bound for California. We shall reach the South Pass in three weeks at farthest. If the feed was good all the way we could make it in two weeks. Game begins to make its appearance, Rocky Mountain sheep, black tailed deer, elk, buffalo and other kinds. There are a good many Mormons en route for Salt Lake. I think we shall take their route; but we cannot tell. —There is a good deal of humbug about crossing these plains, on both sides of the story; it is a regular straight forward business operation, neither a trip of danger nor of pleasure. It requires perserverance, steadiness of purpose and buoyancy of spirits; and it will be but a regular occurrence in a man's life. There is a good deal that is new and novel; a great deal of picturesque scenery, and much that is ordinary; and so there is any where. There is one thing worth speaking of as a great curiosity, and that is the extent of vision and deception in distance. I will give one example: When we were encamped one night a high bare bluff stood right before us; one of our men thought he would shoot into it; he did so, and those looking on waited to see the sand fly, but could not see that he hit it. The next morning it was found over three miles distant.   C. A. BARTON

In Camp, 56 Miles East, of Ft. Laramie,

           Sunday, July 1, 1849.

Thus far we have proceeded on our trip. Since leaving Fort Kearney we followed up the South fork of the Platte river to its upper crossing, which we reached a week ago yesterday morning. The next day we forded the river — it was high and a mile in width — filled with channels, the bottom being of quick-sand, which would sink with your weight upon it. We got over in safety in a few hours, and spent last Sabbath on the northern shore, where we found good feed, and refreshment for the week's work we finished last evening.

The Wednesday before we reached the upper crossing, just after the train started from our nooning, we encountered the most terrible hail-storm I ever heard of. The lightnings flashed, and the heavens crashed with the thunder as fierce and terrible as the description at Sinai's Mount. The hail came with a roar. The cry was, "unloose the cattle from the wagons and let them go." Some succeeded in doing so; but so sudden and terrible was the storm, that, en masse, the cattle wheeled with the wagons, for they were facing the storm, and amid the terrors of the scene, the expedition seemed to be destroyed, and our hopes and lives jeoparded. Many were badly injured with rocks (hail-stones) which cut their faces and heads. I received a blow on each side of the head which made the stars appear. Just at that time, as I ran about for some shelter, a wagon upset and I got my head on the underside, thus protecting it from further blows, leaving my back and legs exposed. As the great masses struck my back they made my old bones rattle. I assure you I never wish to pass through another such scene. As the clouds cleared away, we looked around to see the extent of the loss. In the general stampede of men and cattle no serious damage occurred. Two wagon tongues were broken, which were speedily repaired. The blood was washed from the faces and heads of the men; and when we found no one was killed, and that our cattle were preserved, in less than two hours the train moved on in good order. The hail-stones were many of them from two to three inches in diameter, and many of them irregular in their shapes. I cannot see how we all escaped death. A blow on the temples it seems by such a stone, hurled with the fury of the storm, must have occasioned destruction. But we were preserved — thanks to the Most High; but never will the 20th day of June, 1849, be forgotten by a Wolverine Ranger.

The same day in the morning, soon after leaving our camping ground, nine buffalo were discovered, and excitement ran through the train like fire. Three of them were killed; and afforded delicious food for several days. Several antelope have also fallen before our marksmen, and their fleet limbs have been desecrated to furnish hungry men with delicious soup, while antelope steak has reminded us of the scarcity in a Marshall market. We are now encamped in an ampitheatre, walled in on three sides by immense bluffs of sandstone and limestone rock from 200 to 300 feet in height. A beautiful covering of grass, and several fine springs of water make this just such a spot as we need. On Monday last we crossed over the ridge from the South to the North fork of the Platte and encamped at the entrance of Ash Hollow, through which we descended to the river shore. From that point to this, I will make extracts from

My Notes by the Way.

Monday, 25th. — Warm morning, little breeze. The train moves from the shore of the South fork. We pass over a prairie country 18 miles to Ash Hollow, in which in the afternoon, thirsty and weary, we find at the right of the road a cool delicious spring. Descending the hill into the hollow, the road in one place is very steep. From the high point of land from which the North fork is first seen, an interesting scene bursts upon the view. The bluffs on the other side of the river — the river itself – the Council Bluff's road, on which we saw white-covered wagons like specks — below us a broken country, rugged, rough with its many and deep ravines — its black cedar and ash trees green in the dry sand — all was a relief and delight to the eye, tired with the monotony of the prairie and the plains. As you near the North fork through the Hollow, a beautiful little rivulet, as its source a spring, dazzles and glitters before you. The ash trees, which are abundant, give its name to the Hollow; and with the cedars furnish better fuel by far than buffalo chips, which however in fair weather are not to be despised, for, besides burning well, they emit a delicate perfume which cannot but be acceptable to the amateur traveler.

June 26th. — Warm and pleasant — the train is just starting up the valley. During the forenoon the road passes over many steep ravines, sandy bottoms, just under the line of the bluffs, which are high and ragged. The road is almost all sand, the day hot, musquitoes abundant and unmerciful. The bones of the buffalo as usual are bleaching on the plains. Records are made on them by the travelers; for no trees here can be used for that purpose. We have just recorded the arrival of the Wolverine Rangers, all well, at this spot. We journey along bluffs, properly named Castle Bluffs, for they appear like ruined castles. The bluffs extend for many miles. Today we have traveled 17 miles.

June 27th. — Cool, pleasant morning after a thunder shower last night. Roads sandy as yes-day, the rain has made them better. The valley narrow and the grass more scanty than usual, yet very fine. About 10 o'clock A.M. we came to a ravine in which was water — quicksand bottom. The valley widens and assumes a prairie-like appearance. Met three returning emigrants who said they had been at the Ferry, 125 miles above Fort Laramie — that the grass gave out — that we were only one day in the rear of the mass of emigrants — thought we would see hard time. (They were from Missouri and had wandered too far from home!) Encamped in good feed — smoked buffalo chips, cleared the tent of musquitoes. Traveled 19 miles.

Thursday, June 28th. — Clear and warm; good breeze; valley wider. Crossed two creeks and passed several fine springs. I drink sparingly of spring water, for many travelers have suffered by imprudence in drinking too deeply of them. The river water is healthy and one can drink his fill of it with impunity. I bathe in the river almost every day when near the shore. 4 o'c. P.M. The Court House, a noted bluff resembling the Capitol at Washington, has been in sight, and we have been approaching its front for several hours. In advance of the train, some fifteen minutes, I lie down upon a little rise of ground just across a creek which empties into the river near. One can see objects at a great distance here, and they appear near. Many incidents have occurred in members running off to see some object they supposed a short distance, and they would have to walk for miles before reaching it. They begin to understand it better now. The Court House stands back from the trail about 2 miles distant, and regular in its lines, apparently a huge structure of man. Ahead is seen Chimney Rock, which appears at the distance of 20 miles. It can be seen some times at double the distance; the lofty spire towering up above all other objects. To-day gnats and musquitoes have been busy. The former is the worst. Without noise or warning this amiable little insect, like its prototype in the human family the backbiter, approaches you without warning, and the first thing you know you have been stung; whilst the musquitoe, like an honorable adversary, warns you to defend yourself, for he is after you. I have had to put my silk handkerchief over my ears and neck, and wear it so to-day, for they annoy and leave their tracks upon me in blotches wherever on my long face they travel. 20 miles to-day. Encamped opposite the Court House.

Friday, June 29th. — Warm, sultry morning — road sandy. The cholera swept off many passing here from 15th to 22d

June. Four graves were noticed yesterday and seven to-day, by the way side. 9 o'c. A.M. — The breeze springs up cool and delightful; this is common; almost every day the heated traveler is favored by a breeze that refreshes him, when without it, he would sink under the scorching sun. Approaching Chimney Rock the bluffs are magnificent. Nooned 2 miles from the rock; feed good. The great trouble here, is the distance from the river. We met a Gov't Express from the Fort to the Frontier, as we stopped at noon. They told us the mass of Emigrants was some 200 to 250 miles ahead of us. After examining our train they told us we would get through in good season. This encouraged some who imagine a thousand difficulties always ahead! The scene here is splendid. Many have gone out in advance to see the rock. The trail runs near enough to it to satisfy me, and 20 miles a day is about as much as I wish to walk for exercise. 3 P.M. — Now opposite Chimney Rock. We are at the shore of the river filling casks, canteens, pails, kettles, oxen, horses and men with water. Standing out isolated before us, at the distance of two miles, apparently a ¼ of a mile, is the vast Pyramid with its single spire. The men who are near it look as they do in the pictures where men are viewing the Egyptian Pyramids. For many miles on both sides of the river we see the lofty walls of rock in regular and irregular outlines, as left by the furious winds and rains, and one feels himself regarding the most wonderful works of art which history makes mention. The spire of the rock – the chimney — is about 40 feet thick — worn considerably by the storms. The base of the pile must be ¾ of a mile in circumference; its height 300 feet. The names of many travelers are recorded upon it, and also upon the rock at a spring a short distance from it. A friend of mine told me he recorded my name in both places. As long as the storms leave this rock standing it will be regarded by all travelers as a landmark of an imposing and curious workmanship. The train moves; encamp opposite a cluster of rocky castles. Distance 20 miles.

June 30 — Warm, sultry morning; innumerable musquitoes and gnats. The road is sandy mostly along the river shore. Camp at noon near Scott's Bluff, where the road leaves the shore for the uplands in the rear. All the afternoon we travel in the ampitheatre before referred to. Three buffalo were hemned in and chased by the hunters, in the presence of the train, for miles. They crossed the head of the train and made for the bluffs on our right. Capt. Potts, at the head of several horsemen, pursued them. Two of them escaped. One old bull, after being repeatedly shot, and turning on his assailants, was driven over into a ravine 200 feet deep. He broke one of his legs in the fall, but recovering himself moved on. The hunters made up to him. In the melee, before the old fellow was forced over the bluff, he pitched at Ladd's horse, caught him in his side, threw him and Ladd went flying in a tangent some ten feet in the air. The bull went on, and Ladd was uninjured. The horse was badly gored; it belonged to Dr. Carr. The bull was then killed; his hide preserved, and portions of his carcass; and brought into camp in the evening.

July 1st, Sunday. — Camp in the ampitheatre in the rear of Scotts' and the bluffs West on the river; very warm. 12 o'c. M., showers are gathering on all sides; the thunder rolls; it is raining slightly here; now we are getting a fine shower. The evening is very fine; a moonlight scene here is never to be forgotten.

Monday, July 2d. — The early morn cloudy and cool; clouds of mists overhanging the surrounding cliffs are gradually fading away, as the morn advances. The train moves again; we ascend a hill leading from our camp. A mile from the road across a deep ravine in which are several springs, a man has a blacksmith shop, and keeps certain supplies for Emigrants. In the ravine the largest cedars I ever saw flourish. The man has an Indian wife and family, and seems to live much at ease, making money plentifully. As we ascended another hill we caught a first view of Laramie's Peak of the Rocky Mountains, 150 miles distant, and of the Black Hills. The peak stands up painted against the Western sky, like a dark cloud an hour high from the horizon. The views now from high points are vast. Through the clear atmosphere the wonderful works of nature are seen far ahead. Crossed Horse Creek, a warm and slow stream without bush or tree, and encamped where the road turns round the bluffs towards the river. Distance 21 miles.

Tuesday, July 3. — Warm and clear; a cool breeze springs up from the West. Road along the river, heavy with sand. Vegetation scanty, yet streaks of green nutritious grass relieve the arid waste and furnish proper camping grounds. River narrow and swift, and fringed with willows and cotton wood. Distance 20 miles. — Camp near Fort Bernard, an old trading post. Feed good where we encamp. The Board of Directors decided to stay over tomorrow to celebrate the 4th of July. Many were dissatisfied, and met to tumultous meeting to overrule the decision. The turbulent spirits spouted, and seemed about to succeed. I was cooking; I left my beans and apple-sauce on the stove and explained the reasons that had induced the Directors to conclude to stop, and succeeded in procuring a vote affirming our action.

Wednesday, July 4. — Preparation busy for celebrating; some few decline to have any thing to do with it; but they trouble themselves more by declining to eat a good dinner than others. Day clear; sun hot, but as usual a cool breeze. We stop here in preference to going to Fort Laramie which is only 8 miles distant, for here the feed is good, and in that vicinity we are informed it is bad. 6 P.M. The celebration is over. I read the Declaration of Independence, prefacing it with some remarks. Mr. Saxton, of Plymouth, delivered the Oration. A tent was prepared, open at the bottom for the officers, with a table in front of the speaker. Mr. Charley was President of the day; Capt. Potts, Marshal. The procession was formed and marched thither in regular order, Ladd making music with the bugle. [We here omit the enumeration of the eatables, and other things that were described last week.] During the toasting, a train of packed mules from Iowa hove in sight, bound for the diggins. We intercepted them and they halted, came in, ate and drank with us, and took their departure refreshed. Several hours were spent at the table; and the utmost conviviality and good feeling prevailed. In good season the wagons were all returned to the coral, and all was snug and in good order again. I think this celebration calculated to preserve the harmony of the company; for it has evinced clearly who they are that love disorder, and their influence will be destroyed; for nearly all participated in the festivity, which in its nature is calculated to cement hearts. A beautiful moon has arisen and I write beside my tent seated on the grass. The health of the company continues good. I need not say that mine is so. We have now performed a good full third of our journey. I feel I am capable of the rest, Providence continuing to preserve my life and health.   [James Pratt]

Fort Laramie, June 5.

We crossed the Laramie River in safety. It is a wide, deep stream; I swam it; sending my clothers over in a wagon. [Description of the Fort, &c. same as Camp's.]

[September 26, 1849]   *IN SOUTH PASS, Aug. 1.*

We are now in the South Pass of the Rocky Mountains; all well; cattle fat as seals, in good spirits; have been recruiting cattle one week.

H.C. LADD.

Accompanying the above is a letter from Mr. Ladd, of July 8, 50 miles west of Fort Laramie, from which we make a few extractss

We are now 55 miles from the Mormon Ferry across the

Platte River, and rumor tells us that for 40 miles on this side of the Ferry there is no grass; so we are to-day cutting some to last us across this barren spot. Ever since we left Independence we have been told by individuals going back, that we could not go any farther, as the feed was all gone, and ten thousand difficulties in the way; so far as this point, however, we have found all these stories false; they are got up by the "backouts" as an excuse to cover their shame. Our motto is to go ahead till we see the Elephant, and if we cannot conquer him we will try and go around him. If by any emergency our train should be so delayed or we become satisfied that it would be unwise or unsafe to go through to California, instead of backing out we shall go into winter quarters in the valley of Bear river, some 6 or 7 hundred miles this side, and lay over till spring; but we do not think of being obliged to do so. I only mention this as our probable course in case the emigration that is ahead of us has used up all the feed. As for wintering over, were it not for being delayed 6 months longer, I should like it first rate. We were told by Lieutenant Woodbury and Maj. Sanderson at Ft. Laramie that a company could lay over in that river with as much safety and comfort as if they were in the States. Grass is abundant and cottonwood plenty. Cattle eat the cotton browse and will winter there and will come out as fat as seals in the spring. We need have no fears of going into winter quarters there without provisions, as game is abundant; and they say that by curing meat without salt we would want but little or no bread-stuffs. This emergency, however, would not occur with us, as we have flour and meal enough, together with our beans and rice each man ½ pound per day for 14 months, and meat for 5 months, without killing any game. The above description of the Bear river valley is given us by men who have been in the country 18 or 20 years, and know all about this kind of business. These same men tell us that we will go through this fall.

* * * * You may depend on one thing; this company is determined to go safe and not expose our lives or property by pushing ahead faster than our teams can stand it; or running blindly into difficulties that we cannot surmount.

The water of the Platte here is quite clear compared with what it was when we first struck it, and twice as cold. It takes its rise in the mountains and is the great vein to let off the water made by the melting snow on the mountains. In my last letter I forgot to mention the Indian mode of burying the dead. We have passed several lodges shut up and fastened. These contain the dead bodies of their favorite wives. If a squaw dies that they do not think much of, they roll her up in her blanket and some skins and put her up in a tree. I visited one a few days ago on the bank of the Platte. Some of our boys, a few days since, found a battle ground, where the Sioux and Pawnees had had a battle a few weeks before. Broken bows and arrows were scattered about, and four graves were made on the ground, by setting stakes about 8 feet high, and laying sticks across the top, forming a platform; on these the body is laid out in state, with all the instruments of war, &c. &c. Then their horses are killed and laid under the grave.

In my last I gave you an account of my buffalo chase. I told you I would send you a lock of the old fellow's wool; I have enclosed it in this. We have not seen any buffalo since, and in fact I am not very anxious about seeing any more very soon.

A young man in our camp who is on his way back tells us that to-morrow or next day we will see hundreds of mountain sheep. These are first rate game, and I am in for a few. We have about fifteen good hunters as can be found, and when we are in a game country we live on nothing but tenderloins and other choice bits. — Our company all continue well and in good spirits.

When I get back I am going to fit out a nice train and take about six men and their wives and come out as far as this point on a pleasure excursion. It would be one of the greatest places in the world to travel — roads good, feed abundant, game plenty, and oh! such magnificent scenery; but I must close. HORACE.

[January 9, 1850]

Extract of a letter from H.C. Ladd to Mrs. Ladd, from "Camp on Pitt River, 150 miles north of Sutter's Fort, and 100 from the summit of the Sierra Nevada," dated October 18th, 1849:

DEAR ANN: — It gives me great pleasure to again have an opportunity of writing to you, to let you know that I am well and in good spirits. We have been grossly deceived by going a new route from the Humboldt to the North or Lawson's Pass of the Mountains, making our route at least one month longer than it would have been on the old route; but we got through, and when I see you I will tell you what a time we had. But here we are — our teams in good order — and we are pushing ahead. We passed the summit eight days ago; and it was a proud day for us, I can assure you. We are now coming into the game country — killed this morning two black-tailed deer, a wild goose and a duck.

Our Marshall boys are all well, and all wish to have their love sent to their friends. There are eight men encamped with us to-night from Sutter's Fort. They have been up as far as the Pass, with provisions for the relief of emigrants who might be out there, and are now on their return. They give us great accounts from the diggings; one of them tells me he worked for 5 months in the mines and averaged two ounces per day for the whole time.

Our company have dissolved their association, and are now going on in small parties. I have formed an association

[67]

with Potts, Manser, Cook, De Arman, Pratt, and six others who are strangers to you; but they are right, and we shall calculate to work together mining this winter. Barton, Hermon and Elmon Camp, G.W. Olcott and others, have gone on ahead on foot. I have but a moment to write, and must therefore close.

LONG POINT or BAR, FEATHER RIVER MINES,

[January 23, 1850] 20 miles above Sutter's Fort, Nov. 20, 1849.

MY DEAR WIFE: — It is with the greatest pleasure I embrace this opportunity of writing to you, to let you know that I am well, and settled here for the present. Our company are most of them scattered up and down this river at work mining. They are all well. I own a machine in connection with Mr. Manser, Thos. Cook and DeArman. We were induced to go out of the usual course to California, and take what is called the northern or Lawson route, by which means we have lost every thing — our wagons and horses, provisions, tools, and our private baggage. Most of us got in with the clothes we had on our backs. I managed, however, to save a suit, and have enough to last all winter. We were caught in the snow on the mountains, about 150 miles from here, and had to leave every thing and foot it in as quick as possible. We waded through snow 9 feet deep. Provisions are dreadfully high at this place. Flour is 10 shillings per lb.; beef 50 cents per pound, and every thing in proportion. Sugar is the cheapest, being only 6s.

The rainy season had set in before we got here, and we cannot work but little; but when we do get a chance we put in. It is very healthy here, and I mean to stay here all winter, in order to be on hand when spring opens, which they tell me will be about the middle of February. The winter here is much like our spring – sunny and pleasant alternately.

Please call on Mrs. Allcott, by George's request, and tell her that George is well and healthy also, on Mrs. Camp, and tell her that Elmon will write in a few days. I saw him yesterday, and he had no writing materials. Mr. Jas. Pratt and all the Marshall boys are well and in good spirits. We are going to work to build a house to live in.

I am told that letters sent to San Francisco are hardly ever received. Direct to me at Sacramento City, California.

HORACE LADD.

Through the kindness of Messrs. George S. Wright and H. A. Woodruff, we are enabled to publish the following highly interesting letters from two of the Marshall company. The great anxiety of the numerous relatives and friends of the "Rangers" will be relieved by these more full particulars of their safe arrival, and present health and success, after the terrible hardships they encountered in the mountains. No apology is necessary for the large space devoted to the California news, as it will interest every reader. The letter from James Pratt, Esq., being partly upon private business, shows an apparent want of connection, as we publish only what would interest the community generally.

[February 20, 1850]   *Dec. 20, 1849*

SAN FRANCISCO, Alta California

* * * * * You must have expected, long ere this, some line from me from this quarter of the globe. Our expedition was unfortunate. We were deceived, when traveling regularly in good order along the Humboldt river, and took a more northern route, which we were told was nearer, and that the pass in the mountains was more gradual in its ascent, and safest. We found, and hundreds of others, also, that the tale was a gross fabrication, got up expressly to bring the rear emigration into the northern settlements, to their utter ruin. We were thus attracted about 400 miles out of way, approaching near the southern boundary of Oregon. We had there to scale a difficult pass of the mountains, and thread a perfect labyrinth of mountains and deserts, until we came down at last destitute, with our packs on our backs, from the mountains where our wagons, and teams, and provisions, and every thing that was valuable, so far from home, had to be left in the snows. On the 5th day of November we left our wagons, and on the 8th arrived at Losson's. On the 9th, I, with some others, started for Feather River mines as the only alternative, though it was raining hard, for the rainy season had set in. On the morning of the 14th, after infinite exposure and suffering, I reached the diggings, with Tom Cook and DeArman. — Ladd, Manser and others had preceded us a day. The Camps, Geo. Allcott, Kent, Barton and others had packed through from where we scaled the summit, on the division of the company property, and were ten days ahead of us. Rain, rain, rain, was now our portion; but work we must, for we had got in destitute, and beef was selling for 4s per lb., salt 4s. flour 8s, hard bread 8s per lb.; every thing else in proportion — for even potatoes, beans, dried apples, &c. command similar high prices per pound in the mines in the winter season. We expected to get in with provisions enough on hand to last some time, and then send down to Sacramento city, and team up our supplies; but fate, fortune, every thing, went against us.

I stayed in the mines, working when it did not rain too hard and when I was not employed packing provisions some 4 or 5 miles to eat, until Saturday, the 1st day of December, when I left alone with my pack on my back, which was heavy enough I assure you, although I had in the mountains thrown away all my clothing except what I could wear — for Sacramento City and San Francisco. After traveling for two days I reached the Uba river, on which are also rich diggings, and then took a boat for Sacramento City, which cost me $10 for about 50 miles; but it was raining, I was wearied and had been chased the night before by wild cattle, and thought that the cheapest and best way to get along. I reached Sacramento City, Dec. 4th at noon, having stopped at Fremont, a fine little village on the right bank of the river, some 30 miles above. We had the best supper there I had tasted in California for $1.25. Before we had to pay $1,50 or $2,00, if peradventure at the mines or at any Rancho, whilst traveling, we had it in our power to call for such an expensive article as a meal of victuals. I have not the inclination to send you my journal, or to describe very fully the sufferings I have seen and experienced. Should I ever be so happy as to see you again, it will then answer to explain . . . . I learned at Sacramento city that —————— of Ithaca, died three or four days ago under very great distress — the fate of hundreds who never knew want before.

It cost me $14 to take a steerage passage in a schooner for San Francisco, in which famed city I found myself for the first time on the 8th day of Dec. 1849. As I neared the city, a stranger, penniless, at a season when it is crowded and thronged by a population ready to snatch at the first chance of labor of any kind — my heart sank within me, and I felt how utterly desolate was my condition. I pursued my way on towards the post office, and my attention was attracted to the door of a law office, on which was the name of W.J. SHAW — I went in and found that it was indeed my old friend — he knew me at once, although he was lying on his cot — for he is feeble, and has been very sick. He told me he had just commenced business — that his prospects were very flattering — and that if I could help him while he was sick that it would cost me nothing to live there. This was a good deal for one feeling as I did, and I gladly took up my abode with him. Capt. Randolph, from Ithaca, is here, and is making a very handsome little fortune on $2,000 worth of boots and shoes, his old Ithaca stock, which he shipped around the Cape, he having came across the Plains. He is selling common kip boots 16 to $20 a pair; but for a little hole he is in he has to pay $200 per month rent. But he will sell out his stock in the course of a month or two and clear at least $10,000. Mr. Burdick is here and doing well. Charles Stewart is also here knocking around, fat and hearty, and confident of making a fortune. There are many people who have made themselves rich; not so many by digging in the mines as in well conducted speculations. City property for instance is very high and rents enormous, and men are as wild and crazy about them as in 1836. The office Shaw occupies rents — there are two small rooms, a mere shell of a building — for $400 dollars per month! If you have not heard of these things you will be surprised at the figures and think I have made some mistake! Building goes on here at a rapid rate, and many are vacant of tenants. I look to see a crash soon, but don't pretend to know anything at all now-a-days! I have received no letter from home since I left Independence. I have been at the office here twice and stood my time out in the line 6 hours to be waited on at the general delivery. In vain I have gone there. What does it mean? I must have letters in the post office which I cannot get. I had a letter from Mr. Powell that relieved my mind very much of painful apprehension I had that some of our family might have fallen. What there is in store for me in this land of promise I know not. There is a world of legal business doing and to be done here. The courts we have, the old Spanish court, that of the Alcade, and the court of 1st Justice for the trial of causes, besides a few Justice courts, are crowded and crammed with business. When a City and State government is fully organized with the courts, and when a United States court shall be established here, it will continue to be as it is now already becoming, one of the most splendid cities for the legal profession in the world; for the great question of land claims opens in itself a thousand matters constantly for the decision of courts.

I am thankful that a kind of Providence has watched over and protected me when in danger from exposure to Indians, wild beasts, cold, hunger and nakedness. I have lain out in the cold rain, when coming down from the mountains, all night, without a fire or a shelter, after traveling all day in the snow and rain. After reaching the valley of the Sacramento the roads were impassable for teams on account of the mirey nature of the soil and the numerous sluices and ravines full of water, but perfectly dry in the dry season. For miles I have traveled — for days I may say — over those roads — where wading and miring were the common incidents of the route. Then the exposure whilst at the mines was very great; but my health has continued firm. I have for several days past suffered a good deal from a severe cold in my head and throat; but I am in hopes it will wear off; it certainly would if the weather was not so disagreeable and cold provoking. I know not what is in store for me here. Office rent is, as I have observed, very high, or I would at once mix in the crowd and work myself along. Board is here from 16 to $20 per week; so, if a man makes his board and lodging it counts something! The common price of a meal of victuals is $1. I am here and must live in some way, through the winter; then if no better opening presents itself I may go to the mines. I left them because I was satified I could not make a living there in the winter, and fearing that if I weathered it through the constant exposure would ruin my health irrevocably.

Almost all our boys winter it out in the diggings. Herman Camp and Elmon have built a stone house — one of the most comfortable on the river — and Herman buys all the provisions, flour, pork, molasses, sugar, &c. on credit, and they live very comfortably. George Allcott is with the Camps, and I left him in good health and spirits. Our boys are scattered all around on the river. If provisions of other kinds should fail, they can always, by getting up early in the morning and hunting bring in a deer, which are very plenty about the Feather river diggings; and there are none of us who cannot, if necessary, make a good ample meal on meat alone.

You cannot imagine the utter loneliness of a place like this to one who sees and observes the rush and roll of business turmoil and excitement, without himself being able to mix in the whirl and move along with it.

You see no women here; or if you do, but rarely. It is a moving, jostling, busy tide of man in his most earnest throes for sudden wealth, that one has to deal with here. Rights of property are respected, for the interest of all effects this; but for the tender sympathies, for the "hand open as day to melting charity" you must look for in other lands, where woman has a more controlling and humanizing influence. It is no place this city — now — to enjoy life. The most splendid establishments here are devoted to gambling which is tolerated by the authorities, which indeed could not be prevented, for almost every one, it would seem, gambles here; which of course is not the case, for there must be hundreds here who scorn the vice and never indulge in it. But every stranger, wherever he may have lived before, seems amazed when he finds the wonderful extent of the practice here. Bands of music enliven the frequenters of those houses, and they are thronged day and night. There are very elegant public houses here, but they are all devoted principally to gambling; that is to say, the most conspicuous and brilliant rooms are thus used.

If ———————————— had taken a steamer in the spring and come right here, he would have got hold of the market and have made a splendid fortune; he could not have helped it. But now the speculators, not only in lots, but in goods, have got to be wide awake, in my judgement, or they will be the one's the "Devil takes" to wit "the hindmost", just as he got us who got in so late. I forgot to mention Potts. He, with several others, stayed with the three wagons of our mess when we left, to see if they could not get them through. He succeeded in getting one wagon and three head of cattle to Losson's — the only wagon of our 18 beautiful wagons that was got thus far. It was impossible to get it to the mines from Losson's, the weather was so bad. Potts was our Captain all the way. He signalized himself for efficiency in that station. He had just got to the mines as I left. He said he thought he should be in San Francisco soon, as he was very anxious to hear from his family.

Christmas night, Dec. 25

I am writing this letter at intervals you will note. With all my heart, I wish you all a merry Christmas. When I contrast home on such a festive day with my present situation, you can imagine the nature of my emotions. Doubtless you have speculated much to day of my absence. How little you knew where I was or what I was doing. Over a month yet must pass before you get this letter. I know your anxiety, your love, your inquietude, on my account; and how gladly would I if I could relieve you by imparting, with an electric current, the news that I am here alive and well; for even that I know would be a relief to you. But, thank fortune, I am not now on the Plains, and the steamer soon makes its trip of the many thousand miles between us, and will soon bear to the port of New York this where it will readily find its way to its destination.

Yesterday morning, just before day-light, this city was visited by a most awful fire. To give you an understanding of it, Portsmouth Square is an area of several acres on high ground, buildings fronting it on all sides. On the west is the Court House, a large building in which the Alcade keeps his court, and in which are numerous offices — and the Custom House. On the south is a row of buildings facing the square — Clay st. running east and west between; on the north the same, on Jackson st. on the east, also *were* a splendid row of buildings. Shaw's office is on the south side of the square, next to J.D. Stevenson near the centre. The fire originated in the buildings at the east side, and spread with a rapidity and fury unparalleled. Denman's Exchange, the U.S. Restaurant, the Parker House and the El Dorado were in flames in a twinkling. It seemed as if the whole city would go; but by dint of great exertion, the fire was kept from permanently crossing the streets by wet blankets on the tops of houses, and it expended itself on the block it began on. The lowest estimate of the loss was a million of dollars. Merchants, lawyers, doctors, mechanics, bankers, blacklegs, hotel keepers, and all had to move in double quick time. The square in front was strewed with goods, streets and houses opposite the fire look as if they had seen hard times. Windows smashed and their charred sides evince the narrow chance they had run. Great as was the loss, it will not effect much the business of this place. The vacant lots will soon have buildings on them, in all probability more elegant than before. The wind was favorable for it was but slight, and kept the fire in the direction it would do the least mischief. If we had had a little rain *then* it might have been of use — but we have had now three days of pleasant weather. Warm and pleasant here it truly is, in the winter when it does not *rain* — and there are some such intervals in the rainy season. If my health continues I presume I shall work myself into the practice of my profession here.

[JAMES PRATT]

[February 20, 1850]   *Feather River Mines, Dec. 12, 1849.*

DEAR SIR — I have not been able to hear from you yet, as I came directly to the mines; but I now have an opportunity of sending for letters, and should like to hear from you before I write. As I have an opportunity I will write and let you know that I have got through in good health, and have had the whole time. I have been about seven months out of the world, and am not much better situated now

Since I arrived here I have been informed that the cholera was raging through Michigan, and I do not know whether I am writing to the living or the dead; but I can only hope for the best.

But since I have arrived I will go back and tell you something of our journey through from Fort Laramie, where I last wrote, and not give you a full account, but a slight sketch. The difficulty I anticipated before I left home, the scarcity of grass on account of the vast emigration, we were obliged to go off from the road from two to twelve miles with our oxen to feed, and frequently stop and cut hay; and when we found feed we had to stop from three to six days to let our cattle recruit, and what was worse we had no rain from the 20th of June to the middle of November, consequently what grass there was was all dried up, and for these reasons our progress was slow. As our teams failed we had to throw away our property, until we came to a sixty miles desert, 25 miles without water. There we had to abandon a part of our wagons, as our oxen fell down without number. We worked oxen every day in the yoke that had to be lifted up in the morning. It was estimated that there were from 3 to 5000 head of dead oxen on this desert when we passed, and the number daily increasing.

After we passed the Sierra Nevada the Indians were very troublesome. Some emigrants were killed, and thousands of cattle stolen. We had some of ours stolen. We then worried on until we got within 130 miles of the first settlement, and the rainy season commenced in the valley, and in the mountains it was snow. Then we had to abandon every thing and take what we could carry on our backs. I traveled through snow 18 inches deep, which was wet, and raining part of the time. My clothes and blankets were not dry day nor night for 8 days. Sometimes I lodged in some deserted wagon or under a pine tree, I reached the settlement, where we could get meals of bread and beef for $1.50 per meal; then to this place, about 60 miles; houses of mud from 5 to 20 miles apart, which is the valley of the Sacramento, all under water. I traveled in mud and water 6 to 18 inches deep; creeks to wade waist deep; and sometimes stop two or three days for streams to fall. I arrived here on the 26th of November, which is called Long's Bar, up Feather River 50 miles from its mouth, 90 miles from Sacramento City, which is built on Sutter's plantation, he having sold out. We are 230 miles from San Francisco. The country here is mountainous, rough, and rocky. The weather, when the sun shines, is warm; it rains about half the time; a little frost some mornings.

The chance for mining this winter is not very good for new-comers that have not laid in a stock of provisions before the rains commenced. The best chances are up to 20 to 40 miles, but the provisions cannot be got up this winter. There is plenty of the stuff here, and I intend to get some if my health is spared. I think health the first thing to look out for, and I have been preparing for that. We have four of us got a snug little stone house. This place contains about 1500 inhabitants, both sides of the river. With the exception of a few log cabins covered with Shaker cloth and deer hides, they live in tents. There are 15 or 20 stores. The timber is pine, fir, cedar, and oak.

There are many families here, and they keep boarders at $1.50 per meal; wash for 50 cents a-piece; bake bread, pies, and cakes at $1 per lb; pies at $1.50 a-piece, small and thin. Women and children are valuable here. Little boys and girls can dig and wash gold with a pan.

Yours truly.   A.H. BLAKESLEY.

A number of letters came by the last Steamer from the "Marshall boys" now in California, and through the kindness of Geo. S. Wright, Esq., Mr. S. Ladd, and Mrs. Camp, we are enabled to publish the following, which will be read with

great interest by the numerous friends of the 'Rangers', and especially, as companies are now forming to the gold region by the justly dreaded overland route. It is very gratifying that as far as heard from, the Rangers were doing well and contented. Their extraordinary hardships and sufferings are forgotten, in the prospect of realizing their golden dreams. We ardently hope their anticipation may be crowned with success. We have been furnished with a copy of the "Alta California," published in San Francisco, and notice the professional card of JAMES PRATT, Esq. He has the good wishes of a large circle of friends, that abundant "profits", and a share of the honors of that growing Empire may be his. ____ ___ ____

<table>
<tr><td>[March 20, 1850]</td><td align="right">SAN FRANCISCO, Alta California,
January 7, 1850.</td></tr>
</table>

. . . It is mid-winter; but we have no snow here and no fire, for, although many of the days and nights in the rainy season a fire would be very comfortable, wood is so dear that the luxury can only be enjoyed by the rich! It rains more or less every day and night. In the intervals of rain here the weather is warm and delightful. I sit now in a little iron building which Mr. Randolph has bought on Pacific street, which overlooks the low, muddy part of the city; and in which he has kindly given me the privilege of putting a table, and doing any legal business I may be so fortunate as to get to do. In about a week he will remove his goods from the present shop and put them in here. I lodge here on the floor, and it is quite comfortable. To-day is Monday, and my sign I have just placed over the door. I am now afloat, on a plank only, it is true; but still "I'm afloat" — that's something! — I wish I could send you an exact representation of the figure I cut here in my little office, 10 feet by 12! The ground is half covered with boards for a floor. I constructed my table in a corner of the room in front of a window, by nailing two boards on the top of a shoe-box, of which article there are no less than six others piled up in the room, beside a half dozen barrels of navy bread bought up by him on speculation. My chair is minus yet; for a substitute, I have made a stool on which I can balance very well, after my experience on the plains! My library is before me on my table — it is the "Law and the Prophets"; not "prof-its"; it is a good law, and contains, among other things, the "Proverbs of Solomon," and the teaching of Him who 'spake as never man spake'; who astonished the chief priests and rulers of Jerusalem by his wisdom, and of whom the law-yers and other cross-examiners of that city, "durst not ask any more questions"! I have on my table also half a ream of paper and half a dozen bottles of ink, besides a few steel pens, which luckily I found in my sack, brought from home. My letters from home also lie in my table; there are none later than August! I rec'd not one by the last steamer, but the 'Expounder' came in it.

This is a great city. There must be now at least 60,000 people here. Vessels from all parts of the world are at anchor in the splendid harbor. The confusion of tongues at Babel was never greater than here. All day passes by converse and jab-ber in the peculiar language of the country; and at all hours of the night the unceasing jargon is heard outside the place of one's rest — Spaniards, Mexicans, Indians, Chinese, Chili-ans, French, Portuguese, German, English, Irish and the Yan-kees — all crowd and move on together. The Chinese are re-markable for their quiet, contented, cheerful and industrious habits. They mind their own business and seem to do well. In their loose dresses, and in their forms and bearing their nationality readily appears.

My office is near the corner of Pacific and Montgomery sts. The latter is one of the heaviest business streets in the city, and it is the muddiest and most disagreeable. There is a rise of quite a hill to get to where Pacific st. crosses it. The hill is now very slippery. I see a mule coming up with a pack of wood on his back, for some of the eating houses probably which sells for $2. A small load of wood is worth from $10 to $15 — very small at that. Lumber has been and still is very dear; but there has been so much brought in and so much is known to be on the way, and so many houses are imported, iron and wood, ready to be put up — that lumber must fall very much in price. Board is still kept up very high but provisions in the material are low. Flour sells for $25 per bbl., sugar for 15 cents, when it is bought in quantities of 100 lbs. or so. But the market all the while fluctuates, for the reason that little of anything is raised in the country — it having to depend entirely upon a foreign supply. Many fortunes have been and doubtless will yet be made in California; but much money is also lost on stocks now arriving here, which have to be sold at auction for less than their value at home, after adding freight; this makes business and fortunes for many who are engaged in auctioneering. Teaming is very profitable; but the streets are in such wretched condition that it ought to be. Nobody would envy a teamster who should clear his $100 per day.

I have heard nothing from any of the "Rangers" since I left them in the mines. Kent was as well situated as any of them when I left him. He packed out in advance of the company when we crossed the summit of the Sierra Nevada and got into the mines with the Camps, &c. about two weeks in advance of us. When I left him he was operating with two others — they had a good tent and were building a boat in which they could float down to Sacramento in case of necessity. All the boys must have had it hard enough in the mines this winter; but, thank God, the rainy season will soon be over, and then all will have a better chance.

We are to have an election to-morrow of the Ayuntamiento or Town Council; two Alcades and twelve Rejidores or members are to be chosen, and also one State senator and member of assembly, to fill vacancies. Party lines are not strictly drawn yet, though things are fast verging to that point. City interests will govern in the election rather than party politics.

It is evening — I have just got in from traveling around in the city. I went way up past the court house, which is in Portsmouth square, and got my supper, where I had hot biscuit, loin, hot coffee and toast, all for one dollar! I then went into the court which is in session all the time except Sundays, and election days, &c. and heard a cause tried. You can hardly realize one's feelings, when he sees others trying causes and making fortunes in that way, whom he knows are less competent than himself! It is not envy; but a painful sensation of uneasiness at being a stranger in a strange land, unable to push ahead, comes over one and he looks around and wishes in vain for some means to get his proper position in his profession. I have thought a good deal lately of that text of "Dow, Jr.," "fret not thy gizzard," and believing it good philosophy, as well as good religion, I have concluded to overcome and smother the mental anguish consequent upon adversity, and to move on and strive with such means and powers as I possess, without repining that I have no greater at hand. I will give you an idea of the way the lawyers roll up costs here when they get a chance. A man was in here and told me he had a friend who was charged with perjury, in a pet, for the testimony he had honestly given in a suit. He was arrested and taken before the Alcade, and got a lawyer to defend him on his examination. The charge was withdrawn, and the lawyer had no more trouble than one has in an hours examination before a justice of the peace. His lawyer charged $150 for his services. So you see if one gets into a good law business here he can live even at California prices for board, rent, &c.

S.W. is here, and has about $200, and offered to rent an office with me in a conspicuous place and try our fortunes; but I had to decline for want of the means, or else I would have launched out without a doubt of a successful result. I have two promises of business, of men who have called in my office, and that is something for one day! I count not upon these things, but still they are encouraging. I have begun to write you in season, and you probably will have a good long letter from me when this reaches you, to compensate for the long interval when it was not within my power to write. I shall endeavor to write some every day until the steamer leaves, and you will be able to judge of my prospects. The steamer California will leave on the 15th inst., so I will have about a week to operate for your edification.

Jan. 8. — Mr. R. is quite unwell to-day, and I have spent most of the day in his shop. Having just come to my office, I cannot tell whether I have had any professional calls or not. It is a drizzling, rainy day — just the kind for an election, and I went to the polls and voted.

Jan. 9 — Last night the wind and rain were excessive. Just before I was going to bed the wind took off a part of my roof, and I had to pack out in the rain and procure a night's lodging elsewhere, which I did for sum of one dollar payable in advance. To-day, Mr. R., although feeble, came up and had the roof replaced and fastened. I trust it will stay so. Nash came along to-day. He has just got in, wet. He will find profitable employment as a musician. It is a most miserable cheerless day, quite a gale of wind and rain is raging. The hope of an early spring encourages one in such weather as this. This afternoon a young man called upon me and says he has friends here in the mercantile business who will advance him sufficient money to start himself and me in the legal profession, if we can make an arrangement together. I told him what I would do, and he is to consult his friends to-night and to-morrow we shall know what it amounts to. It would suit my case exactly, and open the way for me to practice my profession in a creditable style. We will see what the morrow brings forth.

Jan. 10. — To-day the arrangement has been perfected, and we take possession of new office on Monday, which we rent at $175 per month, each month's rent payable in advance!

— Col. Munroe now occupies the office, a man who deals largely in real estate. It is on the 2d floor of a large building on the corner of Montgomery and Jackson streets; is a good location, and the building swarms with business men. We bought to-day all the law books we could find in the city for sale. The weather has been comfortable to-day, it not having rained any. But such streets as we have never entered into the heart of man to conceive of — if we had not seen them. But, by and by, it will be dry and dust will take place of mud, and be, I suppose from what I hear, more disagreeable still, for, with the dust and summer comes a raw, cold wind, from the coast every day, begining to blow about 10 o'clock A.M. and continuing until sunset. Such is the climate of San Francisco represented to be! whilst a few miles south the climate really is comparable with that of Italy. However disagreeable the mud and the dust may be here in their season, the atmosphere is so pure that the city, in spite of its filthiness, is healthy for those who have the means of living in houses as they were accustomed to before coming to this land of promise. Many are sick who have been made so by exposure. It is raining again this evening. I must make these notes in order that you may see that "the rainy season" in California is a term that has a meaning. In traveling about the city as I have done to-day, one is struck with the great quantities of rich goods, silks, mirrors, paintings, fancy articles, &c, &c. in stores. Goods are falling in price every day. Liquors by the wholesale are very cheap; and on Saturday next 3,800 cases of French brandy are to be sold at auction by the collector of customs, seized in behalf of the United States for a violation of the laws, on the part of the commanders of 2 French vessels in endeavoring to smuggle goods into this port. This will glut the market still more with liquors.

Friday, Jan. 11. — To-day we got three law signs painted and business cards printed, and office painted, It has been expense out hitherto, but I must say I feel buoyant with hope the more I reflect upon the state of things and my prospects.

Jan. 12 — To-day a gentleman with whom I became acquainted on the frontier of Missouri called upon me, to put in my hands a bill of lading, and converse with me on business matters. He and his brother made a quick trip across the plains with packed mules, being only 90 days on the road — went immediately to the mines, and have made six thousand dollars, and are still digging successfully. He has concluded to leave $3,000, the amount of funds he has with him, with me, to invest and speculate at my own discretion, and he will lend me as much more money for the same purpose, if I desire. Money loans here at 10 per cent a month. It can be used so advantageously.

Jan. 13. — To-morrow evening at 7 o'clock the mail closes, and I find I have written you a good long letter, and that the desire expressed in the commencement of it to send better news of my prospects, is attained. The sun is shining bright and warm this morning, and every thing indicates a pleasant day. S.W. is trying on a pair of boots in my little humble office, into which Mr. R. moved last night, and out of which I move to-morrow morning. He has got a situation in the custom house for a short time. He has been quite sick since I saw him before, but is now better. From the office W. and I went to the Mission D————, four miles from the city. It is an old Catholic establishment of over one hundred years standing. The old houses are of adobe and built in squares, the doors opening into a court. It is here that Charlie S———— has located himself. He has built a house and enclosed 50 acres of land, which he is going to try to hold as a squatter. If he succeeds in doing so he will make a large fortune, for the land is of great value, and will soon be of much greater, for as soon as business men bring their families to reside here, from the States, and before that time in view of doing so, property there will be bought for residences, for it is a beautiful valley, and the green grass and the clear pure water, which is so rare in the city, have charms irresistible.

If you hear of anyone who wants to avail himself of some of the advantages of California, without coming here, by investing money so as to get large returns for it, I am the man who will attend to it. I can make at least 10 per cent a month on all the money I can get. Things go off here quick. Rents and expenses are very high, but as much business is done in a month as any where else in a year.

Jan. 14. — I am writing in our new office. This morning Col. ————— weighed out to me 186 3/8 ounces of dust, as proposed, for which I gave him my receipt. The day is beautiful.

The office I am in has upon the floor a good carpet. The table has a neat spread upon it — the chairs are imported of the old parlor style — the room is just right. A little different this description, isn't it, from the one I gave before of my office. I must now wind up this letter. My health and spirits are good. I shall labor to render a good account of myself — with the beneficent smiles of that kind Providence which has hitherto encouraged us, we may hope to meet again one of these days to enjoy the retrospect.

[March 20, 1850]   *FEATHER RIVER MINES, Jan. 9, 1850.*

MY DEAR ANN: — I again avail myself of an opportunity of writing you — one of our neighboring miners is going to San Francisco in the morning, and will mail it for me. I have been well since I wrote last, and am fat and hearty as you ever saw me. I have not heard from you yet, but have heard from Marshall by way of a letter to Geo. Burrall, in which Edna Phelp's death is mentioned. I have now been here about seven weeks and have seen all kinds of times, but we went to work and now (I mean Tom Manser and myself,) have a tent which is large and good, cost $75, a machine for washing gold, and other tools to the amount of $150 more, clothing and provisions on hand, which we have bought and paid for, $100 more. Our living to this time at least $275, and we have $500 worth of gold dust on hand; all this we have dug ourselves, and no thanks to any one for assistance. The mining at this point, however, it getting to be hard, and we are going up the river about 30 miles farther, to look for a new location. The weather here in winter is much like our April and May in Mich., one day rain and then pleasant. We have had no frost here for three weeks past; we are now having one of the heaviest rains we have had since I came here — it has rained for four days and the river is up at least 100 feet above its usual height. We can work only about half the time, on account of rain, and our time is occupied in going to market and buying our provisions and packing them home. When we do work in the mines we get pretty well paid; some days we get $25, and others $100. Tom and I had a place working when the rain set in, which we had worked four days, and took out $300, but it is now 80 feet under water. The river, however, subsides as fast as it rises, and I should not wonder if we were at work in the same old hole again in a week. Now we shall have to work higher up the bank and satisfy ourselves with 25 or 30 dollars a day. In the same tent with us are D'Arman and a young man from Plymouth by the name of Winchester. We are going into a company, and calculate to go up the river to look for a location where we can build a dam, so that we can work in the bed of the river, as that is where the piles lay. If we are fortunate in a location we can make our fortunes in a few months; if not we must cut and try again. We have just made a contract for 1012 pounds of provisions, to be delivered at our tent for 552, which is about half the cost when we came here. We are about 100 miles from Sacramento city, or Sutter's Fort, on Feather river, which divides about 3 miles above us into three forks, the North, South, and middle forks. We shall probably go up to the latter, and if not suited there cross over to the South fork, and make our location. The gold on the upper fork is in chunks varying from the value of one dollar to one hundred. On the main river where we are, it is in dust and scales or flakes, the dust is very fine and the flakes are thin. I have some pounds of it now, which I wish you had to use. There is no such thing as being deceived in the metal, or taking any foreign substance such as mica, of which there is thousands, but you would as soon think of picking up a stone and calling it gold as that. There are a great many here that do not make a living nor never did at home. They are men who calculated on finding gold put up in purses and ready for use, but when they find they have to work to get it they back out. Any man who is willing to work can average his hundred dollars per week in these "old diggins," where all the cream has been taken, and a poor man that will not work cannot expect to get rich here or at home either. Tho's and I have worked hard. The river runs through a deep chasm of rocks, weighing from 5 lbs. to as many tons. The first day we opened our new place we rolled them tremendous rocks until about noon, when we came to dirt and rocks mixed. These rocks we took up and scraped off all the dirt, collected the dirt and carried to our machines. We got in the course of the afternoon about 60 tin pans full of dirt and small stones, these we washed and took our gold out of the machine and carried it home, dried and cleaned it and when we weighed it we had 6¼ ounces, or $100 in this market, probably worth $125 in the States.

The day before yesterday, while it was raining, we went down to take care of our machine, and while there took up each of us one half a pan of dirt and washed it out, it was worth $9,00. I see by the papers that there is a tremendous number of emigrants coming out to California. I am afraid thousands will be disappointed, but any man of good and enterprising character can do well here. I wish Erastus was here now, but how he can get here I know not. I am sure I never would advise a man who has had no experience to come across the plains; and as for the sea voyage, I don't know much about that. I wish you could see the Marshall boys now; they are all so fat you would not know half of them.. Manser and Thos. Cook, E.S. Camp, and Herman, are so fat they can hardly waddle, and as for me, my buttons are gone from my clothes, showing plainly that something is the matter. I am much rejoiced to hear by the papers that there has been but little cholera in Michigan, and none west of Detroit. I want to hear from home the worst kind. Are you and the children, father, mother, brothers and friends living — are questions I ask myself daily. But no feelings of apprehension have yet crossed my mind, as you are all as well as myself, are in the hands of a just and wise Providence who rules everything for the best, and should we never meet again, let us live in such a manner to meet hereafter.

There is no sickness here this winter, although one would think there would be, as the miners all live in tents and shanties made of boughs and earth, but are healthy and able to work when the weather will admit. Most of the miners here are moving up the river to make locations for their summer's work, and we hear of thousands at the city who are already to come up as soon as the rainy season is over, which will probably be in the month of February. We have no laws here except the miners laws, and there are no "rows" or disturbances. Stealing is unknown, and a man who does indulge in such practices here is sure to be dealt with without mercy. If I am fortunate in my summer's operation, I shall come home next winter without fail, but if on the contrary I should be unfortunate, I think I shall stay another year. The gold is here and lots of it too, but it is not every fool that gets rich the first day. A man that has health is sure of ten times as much here as he would be at home; I mean a laboring man. I can stay where I am all summer and clear above all expense 12 dollars a day at the lowest estimate, but that don't pay, to use a common expression here, an ounce once they call wages and two ounces good fair wages, while 4 to 6 oz, is called good luck. If the water goes down I think I can take out 3 or 4 hundred dollars in as many days.

I shall send you some money just as quick as I know of any safe way of doing so; I could send you $500 now, were it not for fitting out our expedition up the river, as we shall pay all our gold for provisions and transit up there. If we go up the river to work, I shall probably come down to Sacramento city in July, and there make arrangements to send you some if I have no opportunity before. I have no doubt of my ultimate success here if I have my health and I stand as good a chance here as at home in that respect. We have money enough on hand to buy us three months provisions ahead and pay for packing them up to where we may locate; if we get them up we shall have nothing to do but work and lay our money up. There are no shin-plasters here nor "wild cat," and a man is sure of his gold every night if he works. I should like much to have been in Marshall during the holidays but being where I could not play I worked. On Christmas, we took out 51 dollars, and New Year's one hundred; better than working in Marshall at $1,00 and trust a year and never get paid. There was a ball at Lovy's (a trading post below this) on Christmas and New Year's — tickets 1 oz. of gold, but they could not seduce me; I came here for the purpose of making money that we might enjoy it together, and shall not spend my money foolishly. I shall write again as soon as I have an opportunity of sending to the office; I have some hopes of hearing from you by letters to San Francisco by the man who takes this to the office, but shall not be too sanguine — there is a man going to Missouri the last of this month and I shall probably send by him, so good-bye. God bless you all. Yours,   HORACE.

[March 20, 1850]   *January 9, 1850.*

MY DEAR MOLLY. — For the first time since I entered this region of the country I now have the opportunity of sending a letter to the city to be mailed to you. I should have written long ago, were it possible to do so. I came directly into the mines after entering the Sacramento valley, and where I located myself, paper and ink could not be obtained, and opportunities to send letters to be mailed at the city (100 miles distant,) were not to be found. The first opportunity I have gladly embraced. I have not as yet heard from home. The mail at the city has been closed until within a few weeks, and I have been unable to obtain my letters since its opening. I am anxious to hear from you and little Ida — how your health has been and how you are getting along. Also from your mother and family as well as my relatives. What changes must have taken place since I left! — what fears must have been entertained for those who were crossing the plains to California! and well might they fear, for the hardships and dangers of that journey can not be realized by those who have not felt them. I have endured what I should have supposed before I left home would kill any man. I have passed through dangers of every kind; from the blood thirsty savage of the wilderness; from wild beasts, from sickness, famine; from exposure to inclement weather, and from pestilence, and during the whole journey my resolution and courage never for one moment failed. I have lain upon the ground for 24 hours without a mouthful of food or water, with no covering but a single blanket, with a raging fever, and the rain pouring down in torrents, not even the foliage of a tree to break off the storm. I have been for three days and three nights without any food but hard bread and raw bacon and one swallow of water, and but three hours sleep. It was no uncommon thing to go a whole day without food and then satisfy my hunger with nothing but beef. But, I do not like to contemplate these things, and will say no more about them. Suffice it to say, that our whole company suffered everything that human flesh could bear, and succeeded in reaching their destination without a dollar; with packs on their backs containing no more than a single change of clothing. Herman, George Alcott, Kent, myself, and others, packed through from the summit of the Sierra Nevada mountains, leaving the train of waggons at that point. The distance through from that point is about 400 miles. At the summit of the mountains a division of the company's property took place, and new companies were formed. I belonged to a company of 8 persons. Our share consisted of two waggons, 6 yoke of oxen, 2 tents, a good supply of provisions, mining tools, &c. &c. Four of our company remained in charge of the wagons and baggage to bring them through, while we (those mentioned above) took each one charge of the clothing and came on in advance. The teams were caught in the mountains, and blocked up with heavy snows, and it became necessary to abandon everything and push on. Everything was left, and has long ere this, been appropriated by the natives to their own use.

Three articles contained in my trunk I deeply regretted I had not packed through, viz: a small gold watch and two miniatures encased in gold, that were given me by Dr. Palmer to present to his sister on my return, and my journal. My journal I prized most highly. I had taken great pains in keeping it, and know it would have been exceedingly interesting to you and my friends. It contained a full description of the country through which we passed, its products, game, &c. &c., together with the movements of our company from day to day.

We arrived in the valley with only one dollar in money which paid for one meal of victuals. We obtained upon credit a sufficient quantity of provisions to keep us until we reached the mines, to which we directed our course. The distance from Lawson's Ranche where we first strike the valley, is about 60 miles. It rained continually for one week after we arrived at the mines, so that we were unable to do anything, and at the end of the week we found ourselves considerably in debt. Provisions were enormously high. Flour $1,00 per pound or $200,00 per barrel; beans 75 cts per pound; salt 50 cts per lb. sugar $1,00 per lb. meal $1,00 per lb. &c. &c.

As soon as the weather would permit it we pitched upon a location and commenced building a stonehouse. It took five of us about 18 days to build it. It is by far the best house in the mines containing shelves, buttery and good substantial bunks and stools. At the completion of this building we found ourselves in debt about $300. We then commenced mining and have succeeded in obtaining a sufficient amount of gold to pay all our debts, and purchase a supply of provisions for the winter. The first day I worked (Geo. Alcott and myself) we took out $40. We average about $16 per day when the weather is fair so that we can work. It is now the rainy season and we do not expect to make much this winter, but shall make every preparation for extensive operations in the spring. Our present company consists of Thos. Rawson, Thos. Cook, Geo. B. Alcott, Herman and myself. Mining is very hard work and requires the strongest nerves and hardy constitution. You may think if such be the case, I could not accomplish much; but you will think differently when I tell you that I am stout, rugged and healthy. I never was so strong before, and think I can endure as much as any man. I am very fleshy and weigh 160 lbs. The journey over the plains has completely restored my health. Herman has gone to Vernon's after a winter's supply of provisions, and we look daily for his return. If he can find an opportunity to send to San Francisco for our mail he will do so.

The amount of gold in this country fully realizes my anticipations. There is certainly a fortune here for every honest, industrious, hard working young man. Those that come here expecting to make money without the hardest kind of toil, will be disappointed. Men of weak constitutions and feeble health had better stay at home. This is no place for such. The gold is here, but it requires the severest toil to obtain it, and thousands, who have come here with the expectation of finding a fortune in a day, and without severe labor, will return to the States heart sick and disappointed; and you will undoubtedly hear frequently that the stories of the abundance of gold in California are all humbugs; but I feel that the gold is here, and inexhaustible. The reports we had of it before we left are true. Fortunes have been made in a day, and will be again, but they were mere chances of good luck, and of not frequent occurrence. The banks of the rivers and the mountains in the vicinity are impregnated with the precious metal, and with patient industry, a person in good weather is sure of washing out his ounce per day, worth here, $16.

The Wolverine boys are all well, and doing well. Barton is at Sacramento city, Pratt has gone to San Francisco; the remainder are scattered along the mines, mining, I shall endeavor to send you some money in the spring; I have already collected together, and packed away $50 for that purpose. There is much difficulty in sending money home from here, as it is all gold dust and coin, and cannot be sent by mail.

Herman has just come in from the city of Sacramento — he brings no mail, and I am disappointed. He could find no opportunity to send down to San Francisco for it. The city of Sacramento is about 100 miles from here, and San Francisco is 140 miles below Sacramento. He has purchased seven thousand dollars worth of groceries and provisions, and is going to open a store five miles below our present location. I shall go in with him, and we are sure to make money faster than we can dig it. At the city he saw Geo. Burrall, who informed him that he had received a letter from Marshall, and that Edna was no more. You can little imagine the sensations produced by this sad intelligence.

Herman informs me that Bigelow, who used to live in

Marengo, was living at the city, and has made over three hundred thousand dollars within the last year. Write to me often.

Yours, &c.,

E.S. CAMP

[March 27, 1850]   FEATHER RIVER MINES, Jan. 19, 1850.

I have been up the South Branch of Feather River, some 25 miles, and have just returned. Winchester and a Mr. Fish went with me; and we have formed a company of 6, and are going to dam the stream at that point, and turn the water into a race. This will give us access to the bed of the stream for about 15 rods, and if the gold is as plenty there as it is immediately above and below, there will be enough for us all. I am now down at Long's store, buying provisions to carry up to our new location. We (the six) are buying 600 lbs. of flour, at 45 cents per lb., 200 lbs of pork at 50 cts. 200 lbs. rice at 40 cts, 200 lbs sugar at 62½ cts, 75 lbs beans at 40 cts, coffee at 30 cts, tea $2, &c &c. We shall have to pay out some $1200 or more for provisions and getting them up to our location; but when there they are invaluable to us. The great rush of the old miners is to the south fork, and we consider ourselves very fortunate in getting a location on that branch, and I have no doubt I shall do well there.

I have never enjoyed better health than I do here, and this is the case with all our Marshall boys who are here. They are all well, and desire to be remembered to their friends. There has been a dreadful flood in the Sacramento valley, and I hear that the city is completely inundated; the water rose some 6 feet deep all over the lower valley and in the city, drowning cattle, and game, and sweeping off an inmense amount of property. In the city many houses were washed down, and property of every kind was destroyed. I have not heard of any one's being lost or drowned.

Herman Camp is trading in the provision line; has just returned from Sacramento City with some 16,000 pounds of provisions to sell to the miners. E.S. Camp talks of joining our firm and going up with us to the south fork. I wish you could see them, as well as Manser, Tom Cook, Givins, Alcott, and even myself; we are so fat that buttons are getting scarce, as well as provisions. We eat a great quantity of rice and sugar, which is considered very healthy here. I am satisfied that the supply of gold here is almost inexhaustible, and that my prospects here are very flattering. The gold diggings are but just begun to be discovered, and every week makes some new discovery.

Sunday Morning, Jan. 20 — To-morrow morning we start up the river to our new location — and then for gold digging in good earnest. We shall be home next winter, probably, soon enough to spend the holidays, H.C.L.

Letters have been received from several of the Rangers, which furnish the gratifying intelligence that all were in good health, and most of them preparing to commence operations again in the mining regions. We publish extracts from the letters of H.C. Ladd and Charles Nash, and but for their late arrival should have given them in full. Nothing has been written concerning R. Hobart, Esq., whose long silence is still a mystery to his numerous acquaintances and anxious friends. Extracts of a letter from H.C. Ladd to his father;

[April 10, 1850] FEATHER RIVER, Feb. 6, 1850.

However, I have lived so far through it, and have got a supply of provisions in hand to last me some 4 or 5 months. They cost us an average of 75 cents per pound, delivered some 25 miles up the river, and I have made up a package of one pound of gold dust, and put it into the hands of a gentleman going to San Francisco, to be sent by express to Ann.

My health has been remarkably good since I have been here, and that is the case with all the Marshall boys, all fat and hearty. I am now connected with a company of 10, going up the river some 25 miles for the purpose of damming and draining the river so as to dig in the bed of the stream. If we get a good location we will do well, if not we must cut and try again.

I should send for my family and stay here a few years, were this a fit place for them; but the mining country is no place for a family, and the cities are worse than hells upon earth — nothing but drinking and gambling. Crime, however, is almost unknown in the mines. I have not seen a fight nor heard of but two cases of theft on this river; one of these men was flogged with 100 lashes, and the other 150 — the latter died from flogging.

The rainy season is now about over, and old miners are working their way up the streams, for big diggings, while the new comers are hanging about the town and old diggings with faces as long as your arm.

We have been favored with the perusal of a letter from Charles Nash to James A. Way, Esq., dated San Francisco, Feb. 27, which gives an interesting account of his arrival there, and the impressions caused by the rush for gold in that famous city. He says, "I saw Frank Balch here; he came out supercargo of the ship Sacramento of Boston." He says, "Charles Barton is getting $12 per day and found, but it going to the mines in a few days. George Hoag got shot accidentally some time ago, but is now getting better. I have been playing the cornet and violin in the monte houses part of the time since I landed; I got $14 per day at first, but the music business is getting rather low, and I am going to the mines. Two-thirds of the people that are here would go home immediately, if they had the means, without going to the mines at all. Generally speaking, the gold fever gets cooled down in a wonderful manner, after a man has been here a week or two. I don't know what kind of stories the Marshall boys write home about California and the mines, but I think they have had enough of it by this time. If you have any one about your parts that talks of going to Sacramento, tell them to take the advice of those that have seen the Elephant and stay at home."

——————◆——————

[April 17, 1850]   *SAN FRANCISCO, Feb'y 5, 1850.*

——— ———:: In looking over the notes by the way, which I made in my pocket memoranda book, from the time we passed the summit of the Sierra Nevada until we reached the "gold diggings," I have concluded to transcribe and send them to you, thinking they may interest you and the rest of the family. They were made under peculiar circumstances, and are necessarily of the "hasty plate of soup" order. They begin:

Sunday, Oct. 14, 1849. On Thursday last we scaled and passed over the summit of the Sierra Nevada into the valley, about five miles from the point where a detachment from Gov't were stationed. Friday some of our company returned to the mountain and got over some of the wagons and cattle that were left. The next day, Saturday, a meeting of the company was assembled and the conclusion made to divide the property. The day was spent therein and the business yet unfinished. To-day the division goes on. The teams were equalized and the members associated in fours to draw them; each four persons being entitled to a team. Several members to-day packed and left for the settlements — the Camps, Kent, Alcott, Barton and others. We learn it is 400 miles over the worst road in the world, and the Gov't agents who have been sent out here to hurry up the emigration, tell us it is useless to try to get our teams through; that we should hurry on for our lives; and this is the reason why it was thought best to divide the property and dissolve the company, that all might use their best endeavors to expedite their journey. I have joined a party of twelve. We have three teams. Among those who compose it are Potts, Ladd, Manser, DeArman, Doct. Wells and Cook. The supply of Gov't beef here for the relief of emigrants is plentiful and we all luxuriated upon it. The scene to-day is animating — property scattered around, each disposing of what he can to lighten the loads. I have thrown away my trunk.

Monday, Oct. 15. A fine delightful morning. Each association is on the move. All feel well that a division has been made, and all are satisfied with themselves by reason of the harmony prevailing.

Tuesday, Oct. 16. This morning our little party got an early start, just as the sun began to gild the mountains and the distant parts of the valley of Goose lake. Beautiful is this valley — rich the soil — abundant timber on the montains. The lake is a good representation of the lakes in Central N.Y., only the scenery is grand in the highest degree. At night we hitch our cattle to the wheels of our wagons, and keep a strict guard. At 3 o'clock in the morning a guard drives them out to feed, and thus before sunrise we are ready to start. We encamped a little behind the rest of the old train which is now traveling together.

Wednesday, Oct. 17. An early start again this morning. We passed our old friends, who were all engaged eating breakfast, their cattle not yet being driven in. The weather is fine. We are now in the Pitt River valley, where the most danger is apprehended from the Indians. The weather continues very warm. A few miles from our starting point we came upon the camp of a Mr. Smith and family who are much alarmed. They are just getting in their cattle, and have seen some Indians prowling around them. Further ahead we came upon a single tent pitched, and a wagon near by; the owners were engaged in oiling and loading their weapons. Their cattle had been driven off last night by the Indians, whilst they "slumbered and slept." They say they shall spend a day or two hunting them. We nooned at a point on the river where we saw a card left by E.S. Camp from the 'Poney-packers' as they call themselves. I think we made over 20 miles to-day. We encamped on good ground, a short distance from the river bank, where we soon set our camp fires in operation. The sun was an hour and a half high when we stopped. The valley of Pitt River is interesting. The stream here is deep, full of holes which abound in fish. Two trout were brought in to-day; and a dam two feet high across the river near the camp, made up of willows with a mouth in the centre where is a willow basket, shows that Indians fish here on a large scale. After dark, when our camp fire burned brightly, and our cattle were tied up, and our supper had been cleared away for some time, and most of our little company had retired to rest, the roll of wagon wheels was heard. It proved to be Capt. Bailey's team. He brought us news from the Wolverines behind. He said they had lost eight head of cattle the night before, on account of insufficient guard. He had saved his by tying them up, and had started off in the morning determined to overtake us. We were glad to receive him, for he is a noble gentleman and a first rate companion. There were two others with him. Mr. Hobart lost a yoke of cattle in his mess, Mr. Moore also, and some others.

Thursday, Oct. 18. An early start again as yesterday. Every thing all right; cattle look well. After traveling a few miles Mr. Crosby killed a noble young buck, whose hind quarters, fat and inviting, grace the rear of Judge Potts' wagon. We shall have a good dinner. The train moves on. Some one from behind halloes hold on! Crosby has got another deer! All right.

We have for some days past luxuriated on Gov't beef; we would now like to return the compliment to Gen. Smith, or some other high Gov't functionary, by inviting him to partake with us a venison dinner. — Far in the west of us, solitary, rises to an immense height a gigantic mountain, the tops and sides clear to the base as seen, covered with snow; a magnificent sight, first beheld yesterday forenoon. The weather is very fine and clear; no indications whatever of storms. We traveled about 20 miles; encamped near the Gov't train, which passed us during the day.

Friday, Oct. 19. We left our encampment, and at about 8 miles entered a Kanyon, through which Pitt River flows with a considerable descent. It is a rough desolate place, this Kanyon. We traveled 15 miles to-day; the road crosses the river many times, and for most of the way is rough beyond description. Much fear is felt by many, of the Indians; and notices all along caution emigrants to keep strict guard. Last night Mr. McLellan, on our 2d watch, saw an Indian and shot at him, whereupon two others sprang up and ran. No one was hurt. Packers from the St. Louis train passed us to-day. We have a good camp to-night; plenty of good wood; our fire burns brightly; and we keep most vigilant watch all night; and are well prepared to give the Indians a warm reception if they visit us.

Saturday, Oct. 25. Last night we thought ourselves through the Kanyon — after traveling several hours to-day we find we were mistaken. The country has now become more open. It is mountainous; the river is narrow, but deep; a sluggish stream of reddish hue, but has numerous rapids. The mountain sides are clothed with rich bunch grass; the weather is delightful. I sit under the shade of a large pine whose wide spreading branches will afford us beneath them the best 'nooning spot' we have had on the whole route. Our little train is fast coming along, and it is early for dinner — it passes, and we 'noon' in the sun. The valley widens and becomes

[101]

large plains. We encamped on the river side, after dark.

Sunday, October 21. This morning we started about 3 o'clock without breakfast, to approach nearer to the mountains for better feed. About sunrise we stopped for breakfast. We nooned at the foot of a mountain; here are two roads; the one to the left we took, as we saw a Gov't train with provisions and wild cattle come that way. They descended the mountain whilst we were taking dinner. It is another relief party. We started over the mountain, and it took us several hours and some time after sundown to make our evening camp, which we did on the mountain side amid good feed, but without water. We had brought some in our canteens and therefore made a cup of coffee and fried some venison. At night we had an excellent camp fire out of the pine growing near.

Monday, Oct. 22. It is now soon after sunrise. The rays of the sun are shining on a western range of high mountains, and the tops and sides of the most lofty peaks glitter with eternal snow. The morning fair and beautiful; the road mountainous. It is after noon, and the road has been so rough that we have just reached in a deep ravine a stream of clear cold water, about eight miles from our morning starting place. The information we received of the Gov't train is that there is a good camping place half a mile beyond this. The road leads down across the stream, and then a very difficult and steep though short pitch is to be ascended, which our teams are now laboring with. The country here is heavily timbered with pine. Some considerable oak also appears to day. The Variegated leaves of the latter resemble those of home, and remind me of our beautiful oak openings. We arrived at our camping ground early, and had an excellent dinner of coffee, pan-cakes and venison.

Tuesday, Oct. 23. We started from our camp soon after sunrise. Our road was smooth and good most of the way. It soon bore to the top of the mountain, and a long and tedious ascent had to be made. We have just breakfast, and have found in the pine forest, through which we are passing, a spot where our cattle can eat to their heart's content of the nutritious bunch grass, which does them so much good. The forest is dense here, and the weather delightful. It seems pleasant now to travel through a forest when we have traveled so long over sun-burnt plains and rock-ribbed mountains. Our party now consists of Potts. Crosby, DeArman, Ladd, Manser, Cook, Wells, Carley, Ives, Fish, Cannon and myself, and the Dutchman Hank. McCready, Bailey, Swain and McLellan are traveling companions; 17 men, five wagons and 15 yoke of cattle. Dr. Wells, Tom Cook and myself, with the aid of the Dutchman, officiate as cooks. The first three named cooks do the camp watching every night until 11 o'clock. The cattle being all tied to the wagons until towards morning, when they are usually driven out to feed. The cooks do the duty of first watch very conveniently, for at least one of us would have to be up every night until about that hour, and sometimes much later, baking and providing for the rest. The old train is scattered all along behind — some near us — and some quite remote. We are all well pleased with the division, for all are well satisfied that it would have taken double the time to move the great train over this road that it takes to pass over it in small parties. DeArman has been quite sick with dysentery, but is now recovering.

Wednesday, Oct. 24. It is now early morning. Our things are all put away and the most of us sit or stand around our blazing camp fire. We encamped without water, but provided ourselves for cooking purposes at a creek where we dined some five miles back, where we overtook Seymour & Co., who had four days start of us from "Fandango Valley." (This valley is that into which we entered coming down from the summit of the Sierras, and was so called by reason of several dancing frolics had there. When we were there many emigrants and families were stopping for a few days, and the Gov't agents got up these dancing parties which gave a lasting name to the valley.) Our road continues mountainous and foresty. We have very comfortable camps now at night, for wood is abundant, and a large blazing fire is kept up all night by the watchers in front of the tents.

Thursday, Oct. 25. We rose with the morning star and took breakfast, and are now just as daylight well appears almost ready to move, for the cattle are being driven in. We had a long day's march, and at night, after descending one of the longest, and roughest, and steepest mountain roads, encamped near a spring on a plain. Soon our camp fire was blazing. Apparently there was no feed for our cattle —right around us it had been good, but had all been consumed. We therefore watered them and tied them to the wagons. Fish and Crosby went out into the mountains to hunt and have not returned. I was on the first watch, and spent my time in baking bread and cooking beans. The night was quite cold, but our huge fire kept us comfortable. We must have traveled over 20 miles to-day.

Friday, Oct. 26. A fine morning as usual. We got breakfast and started at sunrise, with a view to stop as soon as we we should come to good feed, and, strange to say, about a mile ahead of where we encamped on the plains, we found it in abundance! Oh that we had known it last night. We have nevertheless stopped, and our cattle are filling themselves with a good relish. Fish has just got in; he brings no game and no intelligence of Crosby, from whom he separated. We make a short move ahead again to where Cannon has found plenty of feed, with wood near by. From some footpackers we learn that after we left Fandango Valley, the St. Louis Company were robbed of 40 head of cattle, and a Gov't train bound to Oregon of 40 mules, by the Indians. I am now sitting on a log about five miles from our noon halt, in advance of the train, I should think nearly an hour. It is ½ past 3 o.c. The sun appears to be only an hour high from this point, as it shines warm through the pines above a high mountain. The wind whistling through these pine forests sounds like the roar of Niagara. Evidences of a large emigration thro' here are seen in the blackened trees which have been set on fire, of which we see burning every day, as well as in the condition of the road and the camping grounds. Good feed abounds most of the way; but water is less plenty. In this forest-solitude, so different from that of the plains and deserts over which for months I have been passing, I really take some delight. I hear the wood-pecker rapping on a tree by my side, and occasionally I see a grey squirrel or a chipmunck. As I approach near the end of my long and tedious journey, constant thought is entertained of home and absent kindred, and the desire to hear from them has become intense. In our family — father, mother, brothers and sisters — are they still alive? God grant that such is the case. Months of absence, without one word from them, was a privation anticipated; but the extent of the anxiety it would excite was unimaginable. It is the bitterest and sternest trial of the journey. May I never be called to endure the like again. — We got into camp by moonlight — a stream of excellent water near. The pine furnished fuel. We found encamped near two men who were almost dead with the scurvy. They wanted us to take them through, but, distressing as is their condition, we decline, inasmuch as the Gov't train, sent here for the relief of emigrants, will be back here in a few days and they would be proper objects for them to provide for. They have one noble ox, which will probably enable them to make some bargain to get through even before that train returns. This is a large beautiful plain. The night is the coldest I think we have felt, and that is saying a good deal.

[April 17, 1850]   *SAN FRANCISCO, February 27, 1850.*

    * * * We have been reveling for weeks in delightful

weather, which had dried the streets, and all pronounced the rainy season over. But we are a little too fast. It rained all last night and to-day the weather is cold, and the rain still falling. But it is near March, and we are only experiencing the winding up of the rainy season.

This is the most remarkable place in the world. The city is growing with great rapidity; one can scarcely close his eyes and open them without seeing improvements. Buildings spring up like magic. That which requires years in other countries occupies only months here.

Last Sabbath evening I attended a meeting at the Baptist church for the organization of the Pacific Tract Society, auxiliary to the American Tract Society. The field embraces this State, the Pacific Coast, the islands of the Ocean, and the borders of Asia. Here, where all classes of men have met from all sections of the earth, attracted by the golden magnet, is afforded the best opportunity that was ever presented to spread the knowledge of the Saviour the world over. Only think of the facilities for disseminating tracts and other works of the Society. The flag of every nation floats in our bay; representatives of all climes come here and soon depart again for their own lands. They come for gold — they may carry that away with them, but they will also hear a more precious jewel in the knowledge which brings spiritual and eternal wealth. The meeting was a very interesting one; Col. James Collier was the chairman; permanent officers were chosen, and a constitution adopted, and well timed and eloquent addresses made.

I received another line from Barton a day or two since; he says he gets only $12 a day at his trade, and that it won't pay; he can do better at the mines. He says that Kent is expected at Sacramento City soon; he may be coming here, or perhaps to the American mine upon which almost all who work fail not to do well. I received a letter from Mr. ———— yesterday, who says he has more funds for me to invest, which

[106]

he will bring or send, soon. That is the neatest kind of business, for, although money is plenty here, yet there are so great fluctuations in business, and so many rare chances to make fortunes out of money, that it commands a high rate of interest. Ten per cent a month is the lowest figure that it lets for, and any amount can be safely invested. Money begins to seek investment, and it is said that considerable sums are sent, from the States for that purpose.

It is very fashionable here for members of the Legislature to resign. $6 a day don't seem to satisfy them, and we have consequently frequent elections. There is to be one on the 2d of March to fill a vacancy occasioned by the resignation of a member from the city — afterwards there will be one for city officers under the new charter. New courts are to be organized, and clerks, sheriffs, judges, mayor, common council, &c. to be elected.

[April 24, 1850]

NOTES BY THE WAY

Saturday, Oct. 27. The sun is an hour high and our cattle, which were turned out late this morning, are still feeding. We shall soon start, for by the guide we shall have to make 16 miles to-day, which will bring us to a lake. It is a beautiful and interesting scene here. The large plain — cattle grazing upon it — the mountains, covered with dense forests, rising on all sides. Our little company this morning made Potts our captain again to conduct our movements, and Cannon our lieutenant. We are now around our decaying camp fire, while Ladd and Manser are shooting at a mark. We found Crosby at our camping ground when we got in last night — the night before he lodged in the mountains with a stranger similarly circumstanced, only the stranger had bacon and hard bread which supplied the cravings of hunger. He brought no game and saw no Indians. It is strange that we have passed so far through a country swarming with Indians, where they commit so many depredations and where we see their fires all around us, without getting a sight at any of them. It is now evening; supper is over, and some are in bed; others sitting or standing around our blazing camp fire. We found good feed, and made to-day about 10 miles, encamping without water; but our cask supplied us for supper, and we are to take breakfast before starting in the morning. Our boys shot a brace of duck this afternoon from the shore of a clear pond of water about four miles back, where we watered our cattle. We shall put them with some beans and have a soup in the morning. The forests and plains occur in regular succession. The fir-tree and the pine of different varieties cover the mountains and grow to an immense size. The sky, which, since we left Fandango Valley, has been almost cloudless, is now becoming vapory and obscure. The moon tonight shines through a hazy atmosphere.

Sunday, Oct. 28. It is morning — warmer than of late; the sun is not yet up. The cattle were turned out on rising of the morning star, and are now soon to be yoked for another day's work. The sky is not clear as it has been; and it behooves us to make the best of our way to the settlements. Forty miles from here, on Feather River, we shall have to make hay for an awful desert ahead, and we are thinking of sending 2 or 3 men ahead for that purpose, for fear that it may storm before we reach that point. Our duck soup this morning was excellent.

Monday, Oct. 29. We made about 12 miles yesterday over the roughest kind of a road, and encamped on the margin of a pool, or lake, or spring of cold water clear as crystal. We drove our cattle two miles off for feed. We arrived early in the afternoon. Later, Brooks, Rawson and Seymour came up. All the cattle were herded together. Much camping has been here; a great deal of property left by emigrants lies scattered about. This we suppose to be one of the springs which constitute the head waters of Feather River. It makes a basin of delicious water and shines like a gem in the forest which surrounds it. It is now afternoon — we have just started, but cannot tell how far the rocky road will let us go for our evening encampment. I am now in the woods but a little ahead of the train, and a party of foot-packers is just passing. The forest is very dense here — loose rocks cover the earth, and the soil is dry and sinks over shoe with one's weight, making the road dusty and disagreeable. The weather is very fine. I took before leaving a wash in the spring and feel its renovat--ing effect. It is just after sunset — there are some of us a mile or so in advance of the wagons. A branch of Feather River tumbles along over its rocky bed deep in a ravine before us. — We are to encamp on the hill as the descent is very steep. An immense pine log is burning, which is a camp fire worth having. Our cattle are to be driven two miles to the left through the woods for feed. It is well that the weather is good, and that we have a bright moon to light up these nights. We took supper here and then concluded to move down six miles to the bottoms. We got into camp in Feather River valley where we found several other camps, at midnight. Here was a Major Rogers, who has charge of the business of relieving the emigration. He gave us a description of the road from here to Lawsons.

Tuesday, Oct. 30. The approach to this camp was through the thickest forest imaginable. Heavy hills had to be descended and some stout ascents to be made; the road is rough but some better than we have had for a few days past. It is 11 o'clock, A.M. Some of our mess have gone on 6 miles ahead to cut hay, and after dinner, we shall drive that distance. We have green grass and our camp is beautifully situated. It is on a large, level plain – groves of the spruce pine are scattered about, whilst the surrounding mountains are covered with heavy timber. There is much of this plain that is dry; but more of it is an immense marsh. We moved on over comparatively level road, and smooth to our camp, 6 miles, on Feather river.

This noted stream is here quite wide, deep, and very clear. Here are several camps of emigrants, and almost all are short of provisions. Some have applied to us, but we dare not dispose of any of ours, so far from where any can be procured.

Wednesday, Oct. 31. We remain here today getting in hay for the desert, which begins 20 miles ahead, which is described as awful. Water occurs, it is said, at points often enough, but we are advised not to let our cattle go into ravines after it, but go down ourselves and bring up water in pails. It is said that the carcasses of hundreds of dead cattle lie in those ravines —the result of the emigrants having driven them down for water, the cattle not having the strength to return. Rough, rocky roads, and grizzly bears go to fill up the pleasing description of the desert we have to cross before arriving at Lawson's. To add to our comfort it is now raining; the day is cold, the sky obscured with clouds. Who can tell what we may have to endure if the rainy season should commence now? Rawson and Brooks are here with their teams. Noyes came in this noon with a white horse he had picked up and packed. McGown and Dr. Carr and Mr. Hobart are also in.

Thursday, Nov. 1st. It rained hard all night —cold, comfortless rain! This morning the mountain tops were sprinkled with snow. We started this morning late, leaving all our old friends in camp — some of them engaged in cutting hay. It is a bad day for that business — snowing, cold and cheerless. We stop for dinner at the crossing of the river only about a mile from grass, giving the cattle a good time to feed. Abundance of trout are seen in the river. We dined to-day on good beef. A procession just came off — a burial service — Judge Potts ahead with a shovel — then a couple bearing a trunk — then Capt. Carley, and then two more with another trunk, brought up the rear in military order, with his rifle on his shoulder, then a "cache" was made of some articles belonging to those not now with us. It is night. We have encamped 5 miles from our starting point. It is now raining hard. We have some large logs burning for our camp fire. The road here leaves the river which rises around here in a multitude of clear, cold springs. It is now snowing hard. Dr. Mills is cook on the first watch to-night and I now retire.

Friday, Nov. 2. This morning I awoke at 3 o'clock. Our camp fire was burning brightly, and the moon shone clear upon the valleys and mountains covered with snow. It is a beautiful sight, but one calculated to excite fearful doubts of our being able to make the settlements with our teams. It is now 6 o'clock, and Potts has gone to bring up the cattle. Daylight is just dawning. Clouds obscure the sky. Our little party are in the main in good heart, and what men can do we can effect.

Saturday, Nov. 3. Last evening we arrived at Bute Creek, 7 miles. Our cattle were driven 2 miles over the mountains to feed. It rained and snowed all night. We lay here until to-day at noon. This morning Brook's mess and Dr. Carr's passed us. Last evening a large train passed. Women and children passed us with packs on their backs! We moved on about five miles up the valley and encamped about a mile from water. Raining hard all the afternoon.

Sunday morning, Nov. 4. The snow covers the ground. Some of our cattle are frozen to death! The rest of them are unable to move. We lay here all day. Rogers and one of the government employees stopped and dined with us at 3 PM. They are hurrying on to Lawson's. They bring distressing news of the rear emigration. They say there are 40 women and children behind yet; some sick men also that must perish. Also that Gen. Wilson and family are behind yet in a great strait. Cold and stormy the day continues. The evening clears up, but it is cold. We have concluded to move Capt. Bailey's and one of ours, leaving the other three here in the morning. We all pack our clothing. We have to leave about every thing.

Monday, Nov. 5. The morning is clear — the sun shines.

One or two wagons have gone on. Our tents and almost every thing are left. I sit in the tent writing. My pack lies on the ground. We are going to move two wagons which contain provisions as far as the cattle will go, and then — what then? Some of us in the morning, if all do not conclude to pack in the morning, will go ahead.

Tuesday, Nov. 6. Nine of our mess now sit, half past 10 o'clock P.M., around an immense camp fire, in a storm of mingled rain and snow. We left our wagons and packed this morning, and have traveled about 20 miles. We moved on to-day in the snow which was falling, and had already reached 1½ foot deep, until we came to the last wagon, which was beating a track thro' the marked trees. The road was then entirely obliterated by the snow; but we had the advantage of a footpath made by some just ahead of us (To understand this you must know that we were traveling in a dense pine forest, and as we plodded along in a single file with our packs on our backs, the lofty trees with their branches near to the ground, heavy with snow, we presented a spectacle which I presume if we could have seen before we started, we never should have made.) We have descended far from the mountains, and are now, we suppose, near Big Hollow. I threw away both of my blankets to-day, four flannel shirts, one pair casimer pants, and other articles, reducing my pack to a small compass. With the pine and cedar we found some oak to throw on our fire tonight. We are therefore nigh the oak timber, which we were told occurred about here. It was perceptible how much had been our descent to-day, when leaving the heavy snow we came to where it was scanty, and sloppy, and where rain instead of snow was falling. We learn that the government relief train was bringing up the rear emigration about 13 miles behind our camp of last night. Great is the aid thus afforded, if only to keep open the trail, for the deep snow very soon obliterates traces of the road, and one is as it were in the dense forest without guide or chart.

Wednesday, Nov. 7. We took an early start this morning. Soon after leaving we came to dry, or rather wet, ground. It rained hard all day. On we went — on — on. We reached the Big Hollow, in which many were encamped; but we wound our way by a footpath on a narrow ridge, several thousand feet above the camps below —along ridges — on both sides deep ravines —the rain and wind beating one almost unprotected, for the mountains here are bare of trees, with the exception of scattering oak. On we went, with sore feet, giving ourselves no time even to eat or rest, in the hope of reaching the settlement by night. We pressed on in vain. Ives, Swain, and Ladd, were ahead; next Cannon and Manser; then Tom Cook, Hank, DeArman and myself. Fish had wisely stopped at a camp behind. In the darkness, and wind, and rain, on we went; the road was muddy and rocky — a deep and rapid stream running along it. We kept the road with great difficulty. We finally turned out on wet and rocky soil to get a little rest. We sat until we became chilled through – it was dark, and raining hard all the time. Then on we went, over the rocks and in the mud and water, and in the storm, for an hour longer, when we came to where we were hailed by voices under a tree. It proves to be Ladd and Swain. Then worn out we turned in. Snug together we sat by the tree in the rain — an awful night. We could make no fire, for wet oak was the only timber. We suffered on through the night.

Thursday, Nov. 8. Before daylight we arose stiff and cold, and started on our way in the wind and rain. We came on until daylight, when we found a stream too rapid and deep for fording. We made a fire on the bank and cooked our panola and coffee, and stretched out our wet and stiffened limbs before it. Cannon and Wilson (a son of Gen. Wilson,) soon came up. Wilson's father and family are in the mountains, and he is pressing ahead for relief. Cannon and he concluded to ford the stream, and did so, the water reaching to their waists. Swain went with them. The rest of us concluded to re-

[113]

main, the weather clearing up and the water abating, to refresh ourselves. We passed the day quite comfortably. Fish came up and felled a tree on this side of the stream, which fell across, and if the water continues to lower to-night as it has during the day, it will make us a safe crossing.

Friday,. Nov. 9. We crossed the stream and moved on to Davis' ranche, on Deer Creek. Who can tell the sensations produced on thus escaping from the mountains, and coming into and among the habitations of mankind? Here I found the Hall family, with whom I became acquainted at Independence. I was happy to see that the old lady had got in safely with their wagon, tent and goods. They had but just escaped, for they had only been in three days. I have a very comfortable bed made for me to-night in their wagon.

Saturday, Nov. 10. Started in the afternoon from Losson's, whose ranche is a mile from Davis' on the same creek, on our way to the "diggings." It was raining when we started. We traveled until evening in the mud and rain, and came up with a wagon. We procured some pork and made our supper of hard bread and pork, and of some coffee that was left after our companions had eaten, kindly offered us by a negro servant. We then made a large fire and stretched a tent that was offered us. The ground all around us and under us for quite a distance was covered with water. Our fire was nearly out. In the darkness and rain we retreated to a fire near by of another camp. We helped them move their fire to higher ground, and then sat out the night.

Sunday, Nov. 11. We started on our way after partaking of our humble fare of pork and hard bread. The traveling along here at this season is beyond description bad. The soil adheres to your boots in such large quantities that you have to stop every few minutes to lighten your load. Then ponds long and frequently occurring, and deep sluices also increase the difficulties. We only made a few miles to-day, and stopped by a stream we could not cross. The same wagon company came up that we stayed with last night. There is a strong ox team, and they are merely dragging along an empty wagon. We built a fire and enjoyed about the same hospitality as last night, only being on high ground we were not disturbed until morning.

Monday, Nov. 12. This morning the stream had abated so much that we were enabled to cross in the wagon. Now they also offered to let our packs lie in the wagon until we should come to the next creek which they knew of about two miles ahead. This is very deep, narrow stream. We see a log over it, and take our packs and cross. The men with the wagon had to stay and construct a log bridge to get over. We reached Potter's ranche, early, and having crossed the deep stream on which it is situated, we took supper, and lodged at night in a wagon. Here we heard the first of politics for a long time. The new constitution it seems has just been adopted, and an election is to be held to-morrow of officers under it.

Tuesday, Nov. 13. Started early for Neal's, and having traveled 3½ miles came to a tent owned by an Oregon man by the name of Roe, just across another stream, where we took breakfast, and pushed on to Neal's ranche. Bidwell has a ranche a mile up the creek, where we crossed on a log and went down to Neal's. Here we got permission to lie in an adobe house, and in the evening cooked some meat and biscuit by a fire in a corner, of flour and beef bought here — the flour for 6s per lb, and beef 3s lb. There were several other men in the room with us, one of whom they called Tom, who was on a drunken spree and kept up a row all night.

Wednesday, Nov. 14. We left Neal's for the "diggings." Had a hard day's travel; nooned on a stream 8 miles from Neal's. We then pushed on, and arrived wet through and through at a camp 6½ miles from Long's Bar (at the diggings.) after dark. The owner of the tent was an Irishman. His wife is a little, kind-hearted woman, and slender as was their own accommodations, they gave us the shelter of their tent for the

[115]

night. Such hospitality affected us, as we had found so little of it in our distresses before.

Thursday, Nov. 15. We went down to the diggings and found Ladd, Manser, Hank, and Cannon. We found here that all idea of operating together even in one little party (some being still behind) was absurd in our present destitute situation. We must have something to eat; the rainy season had begun, and each man must look out for himself. Flour was $1 per lb, beef 4s, sugar 4s, &c &c., potatoes $1,50; I do not purpose to go into the narrative farther by day and date — the cost of a washer, a mere light cradle, $60; a tin pan 6 to $10 — how from day to day we used the pick axe, the shovel, and the washer — the little profits and the great labor and exposure, and hard fare — all these things I leave for the future, when we can meet and talk of them.

[May 15, 1850]   *SAN FRANCISCO, March 30, 1850.*

I hear drums, fifes, and a large torch-light procession is passing in favor of Col. Bryant, who is the Democratic candidate for Sheriff. — Col. Jack Hays, the distinguished Texan Ranger here, is an Independent candidate for the same office. He fights a vigorous political battle, but I am afraid he is to be defeated the first time in his life, for he has not the money to spend that Bryant has. There is, also, a Whig candidate, but he will not poll as many votes I think as Hays will.

The weather is very fine now. Mr. Smith, the owner of the building I am in, is now expending $4000 on it by way of improvement. It is to be called "Gothic Hall." I shall have a very fine office when it is done.

Although my expenses are very great, I am making money faster than I could in any business I am acquainted with in the States. "All's well" — the crisis in my history is passed, and if my life and health are spared it will not be in vain, in a pecuniary point of view, that I came to California. I am satisfied that I can make more money in my profession here in San Francisco than I could in the mines.

Herman Camp was in town buying goods the other day; he has a store on Feather River, and he brought good news of our old friends of the "Wolverine Rangers." He says the boys are all making money, and he showed me some fine specimens of gold.

Oh! This is the country for young men to make a fortune, which they can do in the course of a year, sufficient to conduct business in the States successfully. The mines are rich, and they who have the industry and the physical strength to work in these, can realize without any extraordinary luck, from 3 to 5000 dollars a year clear; and where can labor find such a reward elsewhere?

So with any other business. If a man will come here and apply himself to any business and keep a straight forward course, he is sure of a fortune, if blessed with health.

The mail closes this (Sunday) evening, and the steamer California leaves for Panama. It will take away over a million of gold. There is a great abundance of goods in the market and more arriving. The ships are coming in great numbers. Flour is only worth here now about $10 per bbl. There will be much money made on it by and by. Lumber is a complete drug in the market — selling for less than the freight on it from the States.

The city has lost nearly three-fourths of its inhabitants, who have gone to the mines — but then there are enough here yet — a wonderful business will be done here next fall when the miners come to the city.

[JAMES PRATT]

My health has been unusually good since my residence in the mines; in fact I have enjoyed better health ever since I left home than I can boast of for the same period of time in my life. The old chronic diseases, that clung to me for years, have all disappeared. My muscles have grown strong, my flesh hard and firm; my chest and lungs have enlarged, and my whole constitution rebuilt. My weight is 160 lbs. At home my greatest weight did not exceed 147 lbs. If I should return home without a single ounce of gold, I should consider myself richly paid for my journey to this country, in having my health and vigor renewed. I now feel myself equal to almost any kind of hard labor and fatigue. It is no uncommon thing for me to travel from 16 to 25 miles in a day over the mountain heights and down their rugged, steep acclivities, with a pack of 40 lbs. upon my back. But I trust I shall not be under the necessity of returning empty handed. Money can be made here in a thousand different ways, and I am confident I possess sufficient ability to take advantage of some of the modes, and obtain a share.

My business, during the spring and summer, will be merchandising. I think I can do better at that business than at mining; and facilities have been offered to Herman and myself which I think we would be unwise not to accept. Fortunes have been made at the business, and no one engaged in it has failed of making something, while thousands have been totally unsuccessful in mining. Mining is an uncertain business. One person may find a rich deposit, and make a fortune in a few days, while hundreds find comparatively nothing.

Herman has been engaged in trading for the last two months, and is doing well, at Bidwell's Bar, about three miles from this place. He has now on hand a stock of provisions amounting to about $7,000. He is selling from $100 to $500 per day. I shall commence with him next week. The place we have selected for our store is an excellent one, containing over 1000 inhabitants, and situated upon the Feather river, about one mile below the junction of the South Fork, and about two miles above the junction of the North Fork, commanding the trade from both Forks and their tributaries, and from the main river above, which are all thickly populated.

Thomas Cook and Geo. B. Allcott are going somewhere down the river mining. As near as I can learn they have made an arrangement with Capt. Stout, who has a ranche of Indians, and furnishes the boys as many as they wish to work on shares. H.C. Ladd, Thos, Manser, DeArman, B. Givin, and Van Brunt, are located on the South Fork of Feather river, Charles Barton is at Sacramento City, George Hoag is on Weaver Creek mining, J.A. Kent is on the American Fork mining, and J.D. Potts is at Lawson in the valley teaming. They are all enjoying good health, and have done well, considering the circumstances. The boys are all uncommonly fleshy and robust. Mr. Allcott would be perfectly astonished could he be placed where he could see George, as I have seen him, scrambling up the steep rugged slope of the mountain with a pack of 50 lbs. upon his back, and the rain pouring down in perfect torrents. His health is excellent, and a tougher and more enduring boy I never saw.

BIDWELL'S BAR, March 31, 1850.

Geo. Hoag is now at this place, assisting me in managing the store, and will remain until Herman returns from the city, to which place he has gone to purchase goods. George is now enjoying good health, but has been confined nearly all the past winter on account of sickness. The little dog FRANK is here with us, and as fat as a seal. My own health continues excellent. Herman weighs 208 lbs.

Geo. B. Allcott was here to make us a visit last week. He is in good health, and for the present engaged with Capt. Stout in a store. Tom Cook is also with him.

Herman and myself are now engaged in building a large

[119]

store and tavern house. The store part will be 22 feet by 36; the tavern 22 ft wide and 59 long. We think that the keeping of a public house will be the best business in which we can engage. We shall also have in connection with this business an express line, running from this point to San Francisco, a distance of nearly 200 miles, for the carrying of letters, papers and packages to and fro, and for the transaction of a general commission business. The price of bringing a single letter from San Francisco is $2.   [E.S. CAMP]

—◁◉▷—

[June 12, 1850]   *SOUTH FORK, FEATHER RIVER,*
                                        March 18, 1850.

"We are in the best of health and spirits and are pushing our work as fast as the weather will permit. In my last I told you that the rainy season was over; but I was sadly mistaken. It commenced raining again in the first day of this month, and has rained ever since — pleasant now. We have been digging a race, or canal, to turn the bed of the stream so that we can work in the bottom, and it has been a hard job. It is about 35 rods long, and in some places we have cut it through solid rock 12 feet deep and 8 feet wide. In two weeks more we will have the race done, and the dam also, if the water goes down so that we can put the dam in. We may have to wait some time for the water to go down. We were told by hundreds, who were prospecting along the river, that our location was probably the best on the river, but that we could never dig the race. We told them we were from the Wolverine State, where the word can't was not known, and now they begin to think we told them the truth, for our race is almost done. I think it is one of the best locations on the river, and that we shall be paid for our labor; but it may be a failure —if it is I shall push for some other diggings.

"We bought and killed a beef yesterday for our own use, weighing 600 pounds, for 190 dollars, and considered him very cheap at that. I have just had a visit from George Hoag; he is at work on Weaver creek, about 100 miles from here — has been rather unfortunate this winter. He was shot by the accidental discharge of a revolver, and was laid up about 6 weeks. E.S. Camp was shot the same way about a week since — he is doing well now — is able to walk about.

"Manser, D'Arman, Givins, and all of our company are well and send their respects. The new comers from the States that have wintered over in San Francisco and Sacramento cities, are just beginning to pour into the mines thick and fast. I have just heard that Charles Nash is at Sacramento city. I have my cornopean yet, and have music every day.

Sunday, March 31, 1850.

"The snow is melting on the mountains now, and the river is very high. I don't know how long it will be before we can build our dam. Our race is nearly done, we could finish the whole in one week if the water was low enough. Our boys are all well – E.S. Camp has recovered from his wound."

HORACE.

SOUTH FORK, FEATHER RIVER,

[August 21, 1850]   *Upper California, May 24, 1850.*

Your letter, which I have just received, under date of Jan. 24th, is the first line I have received from home since I left Independence, more than one year ago. I have never doubted but that you had written repeatedly, but such is the state of the mail arrangement for California, that there is no certainty of receiving a letter when sent. We are in hopes that it is improving, however, in this respect.

But you want to learn something about us. Well, through God's mercy, William and I are now, and have been since we left home, enjoying almost uninterrupted good health. A few days, on our journey, I was sick with a dysentery. With that exception, I may say, I have enjoyed the best health that I have for years. William is as hearty as a buck. You would hardly know him; he is larger than I am and weighs over 160 pounds; he works like a beaver, and I am in hopes that his California expedition will harden his muscle and make him a stout athletic man. You had heard of our misfortune in the snows of the mountains. It was pretty hard upon us I assure you; but God rules the storms, and all may turn out for the best. I would like to give you a full history of all our perils and hardships, but it would take up too much space in my letter; I may put it on another sheet if not now at some other time. We are now, and have been through the winter, about 300 miles from San Francisco, in the gold region of Feather River, which is about 100 miles north from where the gold was first discovered in California. The rainy season had commenced before we got in. It rained a great share of the time for six months, rendering it difficult to travel or get about. Provisions had all to be packed on mules or on the backs of men. . . . . We now obtain provisions much lower than at first. Flour 30 cents; sugar 75 cts; beef 30 to 40; rice 40; dried fruit $1 per lb, &c. This you may think high enough, but we have done complaining. We have not suffered for wont of food to eat, nor have we any fears that we shall. We have dug gold enough, had we had it home, to make us all comfortable for one or two years, but it has all been eat up in this land of intolerable prices. I dug up one piece of gold worth here $100 — weighing 6¼ oz. We are in company with 5 others, making 7 in all. We have a comfortable log cabin, and enjoy life as well as could be expected away from society and friends. We have been engaged for nearly two months past in cutting a canal along side of the river for about 25 rods, into which we are going to turn the river as soon as the water falls enough, which we hope will be in a few weeks; then we shall search the bed of the river, where we expect, from what has been found in other places, to find gold enough to return home next fall. . . We may be disappointed, but all have strong confidence of success. — The canal has been a laborious and expensive job; we cut it through granite rock from five to six feet deep the whole length. Our tools cost us a great deal with our provisions, while we were at work. But we have completed it nearly, and owe but very little. We have had the worst part of the season for mining purposes. Raining so much, the water prevents searching for it with success in the best places. We have a bank, high above the water, a few rods from our cabin, out of which we have dug several thousand dollars; but it is getting to be hard getting it now with any profit, so much earth that has no gold in it lying on top of it.

There is no society here, there never can be in the absence of woman. However things are not as bad as many suppose. Theft and robbery are scarcely ever heard of; every one feels safe from any one taking his earnings by robbery; but gambling is carried on to the highest extent. Many a young man, and old ones too, will go back after all their toil and labor with nothing. The speculators in provisions and village lots will many of them make great fortunes. A great many millions of gold will be dug in California this year, and for years to come. Wages are high, from five to twenty dollars per day for common laborers. Everything now, however, is, so to speak, out of joint. Too many are digging gold, few are farming, and all our provisions have to come from abroad. These, at San Francisco, are not high considering all things. — Flour $10 per bbl.; sugar 15 cts. per lb.; and dry goods as cheap as they are with you; but when they leave there for the mines the prices increase rapidly. Everything that requires labor is high; if a man makes $16 a day in the mines he must have that sailing a boat or driving a team. Part of the way to the mines the hills are so steep and rough that every thing has to be packed on the backs of mules. The trader must be well paid for his time and money, so that when it gets to us the price is increased from five to ten fold. . . . . If we succeed in draining the river bed, and it should turn out as rich as it did a few rods above us, where three men, who got in before the rain last fall, took out in two days $1200, we shall be satisfied. None of the "Wolverine" company are engaged with William and I; some 20 or 30 of them are a few miles above us, among them are Ladd, Manser, DeArman, Givin and Moore. — They feel confident of success. Potts, I have not seen since I got in. He is some 200 miles from here. . . . . Herman and Elmon Camp are a few miles below us dashing away, trading, running a stage, speculating, &c. . . . Geo. Allcott is in company with a man that has been in the mines some time, trading, mining, &c. — he appears to be a first rate business man, and bids fair to do well. Thomas Cook I have seen since I came in, but I do not know where he is now or how he is doing.

[Rev. Randall Hobart]

MIDDLE FORK OF YUBA RIVER,

[August 28, 1850]   *California, June 13th, 1850.*

DEAR SIR: — I embrace the present opportunity of sending letters to the States, to fulfil a promise I gave you before I left Marshall, to write you a general description of the country, its adaptation to farming purposes &c. My short residence in the country, (only about seven months) together with my limited means for getting information, (most of my time being spent in the mountains,) renders me incompetent to the task; yet I will make the attempt so far as my knowledge and information extend.

The Valley of the Sacramento is from 70 to 80 miles in width, lying between the inland or eastern and the coast ranges of the Sierra Nevada. Its general appearance is a dead level, with occasional patches of Oak; this from its stunted growth is fit for neither building or fencing. There is no other timber in the valley, except perhaps a few stunted cottonwood, and sycamores, fringing the borders of some of the small streams putting in from the mountains. The valley during the months of February, March, April and May, presents a most beautiful appearance; it being covered with a perfect carpet of flowers as far as the eyes can reach. This fancy dress is changed about once a week, the flowers wither and others take their place, the whole presenting a most beautiful panorama of colors, alternating from the purest white, to the deepest purple, with all the intermediate and thousand nameless shades and colors.

But I am told that toward the latter part of June and July the flowers disappear, the ground becomes parched, the grass dries up, and except on the immediate borders of the streams, the whole assumes the appearance of a barren waste. The rains commence about the first of November, and continue with an occasional day of sunshine, until the first of April; with a shower now and then during the latter month just by way of variety.

Rain seldom or never falls in any quantity after the 1st of May. During the rainy season the valley is almost impassable; the whole being like a vast bed of quicksand, through which man or beast when once in must either struggle or sink. When I first entered the valley last fall; I was three days in traveling from 25 to 30 miles. But you can form no correct idea of it from any descriptioin that I can give. It must be seen and experienced to be realized.

Raising cattle and horses is the only branch of farming that has ever been carried on here with any degree of success. Many of the old settlers, owners of Haciendas in the valley holding under the Mexican grant several leagues of land, embracing mountain and valley, with extensive ranges for pasturage — own from three to five hundred head of horses, and several thousand head of cattle. The latter are perfectly wild and can only be taken with the lasso. They are caught, counted and branded once a year. Formerly they were raised for their hides only, but since the discovery of gold mines and the great influx of emigration, beef has become valuable, and is now worth from 20 to 25 cts. per pound at the Haciendas, and from 40 to 50 cts. in the mines. When a beef is wanted the Bucaro or Herdsman is sent in pursuit on a fleet horse trained for the purpose, and singling out one, throws the lasso with unerring precision, catches the animal by the hind foot, immediately takes a turn with the lasso around the pommel of the saddle, and the horse wheeling at the same time braces himself for the shock; this trips the animal throwing it on its side and before it has time to rise the Bucaro is off and has its throat cut.

Very good wheat may be raised here by irrigation, but that is very difficult in particular localities. Corn I am told does not do well at all, probably owing to the nature of the soil and climate.

The southern portion of the country is said to be much more pleasant than the northern. In the vicinity of Puebla Monterey on the Pacific, Los Angelos, the southern portion of the valley of the San-Joaqin, are raised most kinds of tropical fruits; the orange, lemon, fig, and apricot are produced here in great abundance, and grapes from which excellent wine is made, are very successfully cultivated.

The hills lying along the western slope of the Sierra Nevada, are heavily timbered with Norway Pine, Pinon, Cedar, and Live oak, with an undergrowth of chapparal and mountain sand.

Fir grows here to an enormous size. The live oak is rather small and I hardly think would answer for ship building.

The state of society here is getting to be decidedly bad. Gamblers swarm as thick as locusts — drunkenness is a very common vice. I saw more men drunk last Sunday on the bar that I am encamped on amongst a community of 20 or 30 men, than I have ever seen, in the same situation, at a fourth of July celebration in Marshall; and I will venture to say that there will be more men ruined by contracting habits of dissipation in this country than will make their fortunes. That most pernicious of all vices, gambling, is working the ruin of hundreds, and what there is left of a man after the gamblers get through with him, intemperance is sure to finish. In mining there is little or nothing doing, the streams are very high, the bars on which gold is found are under water, and miners will not be able to do much before the first of July. In the dry diggings they are taking considerable in some places, but as a general thing there is not much doing.

I have not seen or heard from any of the Marshall Boys in two months, and I am not aware that there is one within 50 miles of me. I believe, however, that they are most of them on Feather River, but probably you have later information from them than I have. I have received but one letter from Marshall since I have been in the country, and that was written last August.

I am using the ground for a chair, and a mining pan inverted on my lap for a desk. I shall expect the pleasure of seeing you in person about next December; if nothing should occur to prevent me I shall leave the country in one of the November steamers.   [Thomas E. Cook]

[December 4, 1850]

BIDWELL'S BAR, California,
Aug. 20, 1850.

I left San Francisco for the Sandwich Islands the 12th of May last on the ship Huntress. My principle object in making the voyage was, to regain my health, which was somewhat impaired by exposure and toil during the winter and spring, and to escape the sickly season in the mines. I was informed that during the months of June, July and a part of August, the weather was extremely hot, the thermometer frequently standing in the shade at 120°, that much sickness would in consequence prevail, and mining operations for the time entirely cease. — Such being the state of affairs I deemed it far better to take measures to regain and preserve my health, with fair prospects of making enough to pay my expenses, than to remain in the mines and run the hazard of becoming one of the victims that should fall by the destroying hand of disease. I judged wisely in this matter as the result has proved. The passage to the Islands, (distant about three thousand miles,) occupied seventeen days. For the first five or six days, the motion of the ship and the influence of the sea breeze, produced a powerful effect upon my system, keeping my stomach in a continued state of agitation and nausea, without producing vomiting, and reviving to an alarming degree the rheumatic pains and fever, to which I had in former years been subjected.

By a thorough cleansing of my stomach, and repeated salt water bathing I completely regained my health; so that during the latter part of the voyage I was fully prepared to enjoy the novelty and excitement of a first voyage at sea. The pleasure experienced richly compensated me for all the pains I had endured.

For years I had cherished a strong desire to witness the sublimity and grandeur of the "mighty deep" when her unfathomed bosom should heave as in the "throes" of death, and her swelling breasts lash each other with the fury of demons — when the howling storm should beat piteously upon her, and the fork'd lightnings revealing her mighty convulsions, should play around as if sporting with her agonies — when the deep rumbling of the distant thunder should utter her moans and the raging tempests embrace her as in the grasp of death —when the heavens should spread over her her darkest mantle, and the wild winds, in piercing shrieks should sing her dying requiem. All this I saw and felt. The longings of my nature, to ride upon the billows of the "deep blue sea" when enraged by the restless tempest, were more that satisfied.

[128]

I stood upon the quarter deck of the "gallant ship" lashed to the mizzen mast, lest the dashing wave should sweep me into the deep abyss below. Without a single sail, she sped before the raging storm, "like a thing of life" — now rising as upon a mountain top — now shaking as into a deep chasm — now plunging onward from wave to wave as if defying the war of the elements, and leaving in her track a liquid train of fire — now resting upon the billows for a moment, trembling in every joint, like a frightened monster as if regaining strength for the fierce encounter – now shrouded in darkness, so intense as to be felt, and now enveloped in a blaze of light, so dazzling as to pain the eyeball. The thunders rolled like the roar of distant cannon — the wind whistled through the naked rigging with a low soft moaning sound, as if in sorrow; then shrieked and cried, like a spirit in utter despair. Amid this scene, I stood unmoved by a single fear. — I had no eye for danger; every faculty of my soul was absorbed with the sublimity, the grandeur and the majesty of the scene.

Time will not permit me to write you all I felt and all I saw. Suffice it for the present, for me to say, that I saw the porpoise, the flying fish, the greedy shark and the leviathan of the great deep, sporting in his native element —that I beheld the ocean when her face was as smooth as a polished mirror and she lay as calm and peaceful as a sleeping babe — and that I do

"love to roam,
O'er the dark sea foam,
Where the wild wind whistle free."

We made the port of Honolulu on the 29th of May. This town is situated upon the Island of Oahu, and contains several thousand inhabitants. It is a place of much importance, and is now in a very thriving condition. The business is prinpally done by American, French, English and Chinese residents, and consists principally in the sale of merchandise to the natives, exportation of the natural products, and repairing and furnishing supplies to the numerous merchant and whale ships, which put in at this port for that purpose. It is the residence of the king, and the capital of his kingdom — It is regularly laid out in squares, the streets are narrow and confined — and the buildings inferior, being composed of wood, small and poorly finished. It contains three churches, one native, one Catholic and the Seamans' Chapel, which is Presbyterian.

Three papers are also published here. One supporting the measures of the government — the other opposing them; while the third is devoted to morality, religion and the best good of the seaman.

The entire kindom embraces twelve islands, nine of which are inhabited. The principle productions are sugar, molasses, coffee, live stock, vegetables and fruits, pineapples, oranges, figs, grapes, limes, bananas, coconuts and melons are grown in great abundance. Upon these you may be sure I feasted, without stint or measure; I literally grew fat upon fruit alone. The commerce of these islands have been greatly augmented since the settlement of California, which has opened a market for all their surplus products; and the day is not far distant when, they will stand in the same relation to California, and with as much importance as the West Indies do to New York. The climate is salubrious, healthy, and extremely delightful; a succession of spring and summer. The thermometer never rising above 90° nor sinking below 53°. Fire in the houses, is unknown, except for culinary purposes; and light summer clothing is worn throughout the year. The climate however is enervating. The stirring, enterprising and ambitious men of the northern states after a residence of a few years seem to lose their energy, and irresistibly fall into those indolent and lazy habits, peculiar to the tropics. The mountains present a rocky, mountainous and broken appearance — with here and there a beautiful valley, made melodious with the incessant murmuring of clear running brooks, and teeming with sugar-cane, patches of the tarra — vegetable gardens, and extensive groves of the cocoa and plaintain — while upon the mountain sides are seen numerous flocks of goats, with their kids gamboling about them in playful innocence and perfect security. Large herds of cattle are seen quietly cropping the rich verdure, or lying upon some grassy mound beneath cooling shade; while the mustang is roaming to and fro, in his restlessness. — The music of birds is only wanting to render these vallies truly enchanting. But few of these islands are inhabited, or even visited by any of the bird species, and while gazing upon their evergreen hills and vallies you involuntarily feel the want of something to fill up the picture and enliven the scene. The native inhabitants are above the medium size, well formed strong and athletic. They resemble in appearance both the Indian and the Negro. Like the Indian the forehead is high, exhibiting intellect, the eye expressive and the cheek bones prominent. Like the Negro, the nose is somewhat flattened, the lips thick, the neck short and the foot flat. Their hair is jet black, (sometimes curly, but not wooly) and their beards thick and coarse. The females are not altogether wanting in beauty, possessing large black full eyes of expression —beautiful white teeth, regular features, and forms fully developed. They have never been injured by the detestable fashions of civilization, which consign yearly, to the grave more females than all other diseases combined — but have grown up as God and nature intended they should, and a constitution capable of endurance.

The complexion of the natives vary from a light olive to a jet black. Their food consists of principally of poe, fish and fruit. The poe is made of the tarra root — the root is first roasted or boiled, then mashed fine and combined with water until it has the consistency of soft dough, then placed in a proper vessel to sour — after which it is eaten without farther preparation. This constitutes their staple food and very nutritious. They consume their fish raw or merely dried in the sun. Many

[131]

of their habits and customs are peculiar; at present I can mention a few. The dress of those residing in the country is simple. That of the males consisting of nothing more than a shirt, and in many instances naught but a piece of cotton cloth tied around their loins; while that of the females consists of a single dress of calico or sheeting, made after the fashion of a woman's night dress. Those residing in the cities and villages, dress much better and with more taste, adopting to a certain degree the fashions of the whites. They are extremely fond of gay and gaudy colors, and when fully decked out in their finery they present a fantastic appearance, combining the sublime with the ridiculous.' It is no uncommon sight to see a native female enrobed in a gown made like a night dress, plaited into a neck yoke — like the neck yoke of a shirt, without waist or collar — of the most superb pink, scarlet, blue, green or purple chinese silk — without stockings or shoes or head covering of any description — with the bosom bare and carrying over her head one of the most magnificent, heavy fringed chinese parisols you ever witnessed — while her under dress consisted of nothing more than a coarse chemise. They never set upon stools or chairs, but always squat or lay in a reclined position upon the ground or floor. They are with very few exceptions unchaste and entirely wanting of virtue. Commencing their career of prostitution frequently at the age of nine years and continuing it until death. The effect of this vice has been very deleterious to the native growth of the islands, so much so that the increase by birth falls far short of the decrease by death. The native population has fallen off some twelve thousand within the past few years.

The women indulge much in horse back riding, of which they are extremely fond. They ride astride like a man, and upon a man's saddle. Their riding dress consists of the silk gown described above, together with a small loose crowned panama hat braided with a wide ribbon, a silk scarf tied around the neck, and light stockings and shoes upon their feet. In preparing to ride, they pass a long scarf around the body, cross it upon the back, bring the two ends in front again, then wind each end of the scarf round and round each leg, lapping it each time, until it reaches the ankle when it is fastened on the outside by a pin, thus forming a kind of pants, and leaving about ten inches of the fringed ends to hang over the feet and stirrups. Saturday is their sporting day, on the afternoon of which hundreds may be seen bounding through the streets and lanes, urging their animals to their utmost speed, while their numerous colored hat ribbons, scarfs and dresses flutter in the breeze presenting a scene truly novel when witnessed for the first time. They are excellent riders, and very expert in managing their horses. They are (male and female,) excessively fond of bathing and swimming in the sea. For this they are particularly noted. No nation can compare with them in the art of diving or navigating their bodies in the water. It is said of them that they will descend into the sea, fight and kill the shark in his own element with no other weapon than a common butcher knife. I have frequently seen the females swim out to the shipping in the outer harbor a distance of two miles, with their clothing fastened upon top of their heads when the sea ran so high as to render the passage of the ship's small boats to the shore dangerous. They think that leaping from the main top yard, or diving under the bottom of a large 750 ton ship drawing 14 feet of water, as no uncommon feat. Hundreds of both sexes may be seen daily sporting among the shipping in the harbor of Honolulu. The females usually bath in their chemise, which are cut low in the neck, made with short sleeves and reaching just below the knee.

The native dwellings are constructed of poles, small rods and grass. The frame work is constructed of light poles, upon this small rods are fastened horizontally, from two to four inches apart, with small cord. The grass is braided into long strips or mats, about 14 inches in width, with a long knap in

the out side. With this preparation, the entire structure is covered and secured, at short intervals, by small cord, to the
rods. The process of covering commences at the bottom, so
that the knap or fringe of each succeeding mat, overlaps the
one below; rendering the whole edifice perfectly tight. Numbers of these buildings are fitted up with windows and doors,
lined on the inside with light colored goods, and floored with
coarse matting. They are pleasant and very comfortable residences. These islands are destitute of building materials, and
entirely depend upon foreign importation, for a supply. House
frames, brick and lumber are imported from the States, Oregon, China and Sidney, (Van Diemans land.) The consequence
is that the ability to build good frame or brick buildings rest
only with the wealthy few. These islands, since their first discovery by Capt. Cook, have rapidly advanced in civilization.
Schools and churches have been established. Agriculture very
materially improved. The arts and sciences taught to some
extent, and a substantial government formed under a whole-
some code of laws. This has been done through American
and foreign missionary effort. The prominent functionaries of
the government are whites. The minister of the interior (Mr.
Wilie,) is an Englishman; the minister of finance, (Mr. Judd,)
and the private secretary, (Mr. Young,) are Americans.

The king is about the medium size, stout and muscular,
and between 50 and 60 years of age; he is educated — speaks
the English well, and is said to be possessed of good abilities.
He dresses after the fashion of Americans, very plain but rich.
He wears no ornaments, except a gold crown, pinned to the
left lapel of his coat, as a distinction of royalty.

The queen is a large fat dumpy body, fond of ornaments
and dress. The heirs apparent to the crown, are now in France
finishing their education. During my residence at Honolulu,
I visited the king's palace and gardens, the fort, counsel halls,
and many other public places, which I should take pleasure

in describing to you, but must for the present refrain, lest I weary you with too lengthy communication.

* * * * I sailed from the port of Honolulu on the 20th of July in the ship 'Cachalot,' from Panama, bound for the port of San Francisco. She was obliged to put in to port for a supply of water. The weather during the passage, was on the whole pleasant; but the crowded state of the ship (there being 163 passengers on board,) made the nights very disagreeable. Rude berths were fitted up between decks, for the accommodation of the passengers, to which there was no egress or ingress for air, except the two main hatches. The fare was miserable in the extreme. For breakfast we have boiled beef or pork, coffee and sea bread. The bread old, black and hard as flint, and literally filled with worms. For several days I could not eat a mouthful of it. In a short time, however, I became used to it, so that I could knock a spoonful of worms and bugs out of it, soak it in my coffee, and partake of it with quite a relish. For dinner we had beans, and bean soup for supper, rice, molasses and tea. This was the daily routine of fare, except Sundays and Wednesdays, when for dinner we were served with boiled dough, called duff, black and heavy with molasses. The meat was very salty and not more than half cooked. The tea was perfect slop — the molasses full of sticks and dirt — the rice filled with hulls and the beans spoiled by being mixed with pumpkin and squash. The bread and duff I have already described. The only passable article was the coffee and sugar. The voyage on the whole, however, was agreeable, enlivened by frequent fights among the passengers, who were principally from the southern states — the excitment produced by the sight of whales in the immediate vicinity of the ship — games of checkers, chess, cards, music, singing, &c., &c. I made on board the acquaintance of several southern men, of whom I learned more of the character, customs and institutions of the south, than could be learned, a resident of the north in a lifetime. A thousand little incidents occurred during the passage, the relation of which I shall defer until I can present them in a more amusing manner, than upon paper. I arrived at San Francisco after being upon the briny deep 22 days. From Sacramento to Marysville a distance of about 220 miles I came by steam. The distance from San Francisco city is 150 miles up the Sacramento river. From Sacramento city to Marysville the distance is about 65 or 70 miles. Marysville is situated upon the Feather river near its junction with the Sacramento. From Marysville to Bidwell's Bar the distance is about 40 miles. That latter distance I was obliged to make on foot, there being no public conveyance. On my arrival at Bidwell's Bar, I found matters in a very deplorable situation. Extensive mining operations being gone into in constructing dams and digging races for the purpose of making dry the bed of the river. The bed of the river was supposed to be exceedingly rich with gold. Persons having made a good location for daming the river, were already looked upon as rich. Shares in these locations being in excellent demand, and brought an enormous price. Thousands expended in constructing their works every dollar they had made the previous season, besides increasing debts to a heavy amount. The experiment proved almost a total failure; and I venture to say that nine out of ten of the miners upon Feather river are (as we term it,) dead broke — without a single dollar and deeply in debt. The same result, to a great extent was experienced on the Yuba river, and the American fork. The effect of this 'gold failure' has been severely felt in every department of trade. In anticipation of a rich harvest of gold large stocks of goods were ordered from the states, extensive credit given to the country merchants, and by them, to the miners. The failure at one end of the chain affects the whole — and already heavy failures in the cities have taken place, which is but a prelude to many more. Speculation during the summer has run high. — Cities and villages have been built up as it were in a day. The times of 1835-6 have been and are being reenacted in California on a much more extended scale. Everything has assumed a ficticious value. But a crisis is fast approaching, and when it arrives it will be a terrible one. Already labor has decreased from 16 to 3 dollars per day, and other things in proportion. The idea of making a fortune in California in a few days, at least for the future, is ridiculous. It requires time, perserverance and economy, as in any other country, and those who are comfortably situated at home, had better by far remain where they are. Where one succeeds in making a fortune, ten entirely fail; and thousands will return to the states pennyless as well as disheartened for life. — The representations which I am now making may appear to contradict almost in toto the accounts you receive in the public newspapers, but such is not the case. The public prints only publish the success of the few, while the thousand failures are unnoticed. It is only necessary for me to mention one fact coming under my observation to illustrate this. Upon Feather river one claim situated about eight miles from this place, proved exceedingly rich. The claim was owned by nine persons, each of which within a few days took out a fortune, ($8,000 each,) sold out their shares for twelve or fourteen thousand more, and left for the states. This circumstance was heralded through all the papers in the state. As each arrived at San Francisco on his way home, the papers would announce that Mr. So and so, had just arrived from the mines on Feather river with ten or twelve thousand dollars in gold dust which he had accumulated in a short space of time; while at the same time, not less than six thousand on the same river had entirely failed in their mining operations of which nothing was said in the public prints.

Success in mining is a matter of luck or chance. One may stumble upon a fortune, while hundreds will only make daily wages. That there is an abundance of gold in this country I have no doubt; on the contrary, I am fully convinced that the mines will not be exhausted during my life time. It is found diffused throughout an extensive section of the country, but not in such quantities as to secure fortunes to individual effort in short periods of time. When machinery combined with capital is extensively employed, mining will be a successful business. The mines of California are her main dependence for years to come. She cannot become an agricultural country for lack of rain. Her vallies are rich, and produce a heavy growth; but this dries up by the heat of the sun early in the season. — Stock, however, seem to thrive and fatten upon dry grass as well as upon the green.

This is country in which I should be very unwilling to make a permanent residence. In fact I would as soon think of committing suicide as to bring a family within the influence of the moral degradation of California. Vice of every description strides through the whole country, with bold front, in open day. Gambling and drinking are carried to great excess. Every public house is filled with monte, faro and rolette tables, both in the cities and in the mines. Immense fortunes frequently change hands in one night. Around these tables disputes frequently occur, which end in the death of one or two persons. I think I do not exaggerate when I say, that nine tenths of the population of California gamble, more or less; and that nineteen twentieths are in the habit of drinking. The large cities are filled with prostitutes from the U. States, Europe, Chili and the Sandwich Islands, who carry on their nefarious business without restraint. It is not an unfrequent thing to see women engaged with gamblers, dealing monte, &c., in the saloons of the most popular houses. Cock fighting, bull fighting, and horse racing, are already numbered among the fashionable amusements of this country. The influence of this state of society is pernicious in the extreme and very few escape it. I am myself acquainted with instances of the total ruin of the morals of numerous persons, who were eminently pious and of irreproachable character in the States. I might mention the names of two clergymen, who were deservedly

[138]

popular at home, and are now addicted to drinking, swearing, & c. &c. One of these you have heard advocating the cause of temperance in strains of eloquence from the pulpit of the stone church in your place. I know another, who at home was a deacon of the Baptist church, now engaged exclusively in gambling. It is a singular fact, that those who made the strongest professions of morality and religion at home, sink the deepest into vice and iniquity here. Did I wish to place a family where they could be the soonest schooled in vice, preparatory to the hangman's rope, the prison's chains, or the torments of hell, I should certainly bring them to this country. What I am now saying in relation to the society of this country is said in general terms. There are some exceptions. — Churches have been established in some of the cities, and a healthier state of morals inculcated. There appears to be a determination on the part of the government functionaries to execute the laws, which on the whole are salutary; but this can be done only to a limited extent. Judge Lynch still reigns supreme in the more remote parts of the country.

Capt. J.D. Potts is located in the Sacramento valley, on a ranche, in co-partnership with Mr. Davis. They are engaged in raising stock, trading, &c. The distance from this point is about 30 miles. How he has succeeded, and what his future prospects are, I am unable to say. Geo. B. Alcott is still with Capt. Stout on Feather river, 12 miles below this. Thos. Cook is now with him. Cook has been during the summer operating upon the Yuba — was sick part of the time, and did not make more than $200 or $300. He talks of going to Sacramento city, and engaging in business with his cousin Sam, who has accumulated between $1500 and $2000. Joshua Cook, Sam's brother, has gone home, taking with him about the same amount. Randall Hobart and William are at work upon the south fork of this river, about 12 miles above this. The claim they have been engaged upon I have been informed has failed, and they have made nothing. I have not seen either of them since they went into the mines, but I frequently hear from them; they are enjoying good health. The claim of H.C. Ladd, in which Thos. Manser, S.S. DeArman, B. Givins, &c., were engaged, failed — after which Ladd purchased an interest in the Oskaloosa bar, out of which he will make something. Noyes is somewhere in the mountains —at what point I am unable to state. The last I heard from him he was well, but had made little. S.S. DeArman and Lewis Winchester his partner are both dead. Mr. Winchester was from Plymouth, Wayne co. Thos. Manser is with John Nichols about 8 miles from this on the road to Maryville. He has made nothing. Geo. W. Hoag is boarding with me at this place. He is the deputy sheriff of this county — does considerable business —is quite popular, and if things turn as we have reason to suppose they will, he will be in the road to wealth. I think his prospects are flattering. His health is good, as well as that of the dog Frank. Geo. says he is bound to take Frank home if he lives, even if it should cost him one hundred dollars. He is the only dog now in existence that commenced the perilous journey over the plains with the Wolverine Rangers.

Of those who came over the plains this season, I have seen Sol. Platner, Geo. Bostock, Z. Sidmore, Wm. Brace, John and Chas. Nichols, Robinson, Israel Harvey, and Mr. Chandler. Platner is keeping public house at Marysville. Linus West is with him, John and Charles Nichols have purchased a ranch about 8 miles from this place, on the road to Marysville. Chandler is with them. They are doing a good business. Geo. Bostock is in the dry diggings. Wm. Brace has been extremely lucky. He struck upon a rich vein in the dry diggings, and has already taken out $4,000, and has been offered $2,000 more for his location. I. Harvey is at work on the Oskaloosa bar for seven dollars per day, and found. Henry Hahn is at Sacramento city, engaged in his profession — how he is succeeding I am unable to say. Wm. Thornton and John Cuykendall are, as I have been informed, at Hangtown.   [Elmon S. Camp]

[April 25, 1851]

I left my old residence at Bidwell's Bar about the middle of November last, for this point, in company with nine others. The weather was warm and pleasant through the day, but cold during the night. The route was an unfrequented one, leading over high ranges of mountains, and through thick masses of chapperel. The climbing of these mountains, especially with a load of forty pounds upon your shoulders, is a task the most fatiguing — at least I found it so. In passing the chapperel, the utmost patience and perserverence is required. Your progress is slow, it being necessary in many places to cut an opening through with your knife. The tearing of your clothes is an expected contingency, and should you escape with a whole skin you have cause for congratulation.

We arrived at this point on the evening of the fifth day, well wearied with our journey. This Bar is situated on the N.E. branch of the north fork of Feather river. It is enclosed on every side by lofty mountains, through which the river 'canon', whose summits are frequently hid from view by the clouds, which rest mid way upon its sides. The rays of the sun are obstructed so as not to reach us until late in the fore part of the day, and on many places their genial influence is never felt. The height of these mountains has never been ascertained. The only criterion by which we can judge is from time occupied in scaling them. I am now gazing upon one from my cabin door over which the trail runs that leads from this bar to the settlements below. It is the easiest and most feasible route that leads out of these diggins, yet it requires an early start in the morning to reach its summit by two o'clock P.M., and that too by those who are inured to the hardships of a mountain life. On my arrival here I found a population of about 300 persons, comfortably situated for the winter, with good warm cabins and an abundant supply of provisions. Two miles above this was another settlement on Rich bar, and another, one and a half miles below on Saylors bar. Provisions were extremely high. Flour, corn meal, pork, one dollar per pound. Dried apples, beans, rice $1.25 per pound. Hams, coffee, sugar, salt, &c. $1.50 per pound. Butter, cheese, candles, soap, saleratus, &c. $3.00 per pound, and all other articles in proportion. Board, by the day, $7.50; liquor by the glass fifty cents; cigars fifty cents each. Molasses $10 and vinegar $8 per gallon. The prospects for mining during the winter were not very flattering. It was supposed that we should be visited by heavy falling snow, which would force us to 'burrow' during the greater part of the time. It was even predicted that we should all be buried up in snow, and perish. The predictions were far from being verified. The winter has been uncommonly pleasant — so much so that the natives are themselves surprised and attribute it to the influence of the white man. During the past summer we were visited by several showers of rain, an occurrence unknown in California for a long series of years. The natives then said with superstitious fear, the 'pale face' bring the cool breeze and the rain. The unusual calmness of this winter leads them to exclaim. 'The sun shineth on the path of the pale face, and the snow fleeth away before him.' Indeed the winter in this country has been less stormy and quite as pleasant as in any of the States. The result in the valley, however, is ruinous. A sufficiency of water has not fallen to moisten the earth and cause vegetation to thrive — feed for stock is, in consequence, greatly reduced. Many of the large Ranche owners, I have been informed, are already engaged in driving their stock to the mountain vallies in order to save them. This portion of California is heavily timbered, principally with pine, cedar, fir and spruce. In some portions groves of oak may be seen. The mountains are steep, rugged and rocky — sometimes covered with a red soil, but sustaining no vegetation, except the heavy timber above mentioned. Between the high ranges of these mountains are valleys well watered, and bearing upon their bosoms a rich, luxuriant growth of vegetation.

The society of this region consists of — of — males and — men. Not a white woman resides within fifty miles. Would it be at all a matter of wonder if we should become as boorish in our manners as untutored heathens, and lose all pride of personal appearance.

The success of the miners in these diggings has been anything but uniform; some have merely paid their expenses, while a few have made fortunes. The greater portion have been making what is now considered fair wages, viz from 8 to 12 dollars per day. Out of this they can lay up about five dollars. This portion of the mining region is now considered the richest and most extensive of any in California. The excitement in the valley below caused by the wonderful success of a few persons on this and Rich bar is bringing crowds to this vicinity. Scores are daily arriving, and it is reported that from 15 to 20 thousand persons are making preparations to start as soon as pack animals can get through. Disappointment awaits the great mass—a small portion only will have their anticipation realized.

Mining is an uncertain business. You may toil a week without finding a single scale. The next day you may strike a lead — a small amount or an independent fortune. Hundreds have toiled like slaves on this and other bars in the immediate vicinity during the winter, and failed in finding more than a sufficient amount to pay expenses. Some eight or ten companies (containing in all about fifty men) have been fortunate in striking rich leads, and are now taking their "piles." Some of these claims have paid as much as three pounds of gold dust to the man per day. Sixty-two ounces have been taken out of one pan of earth. The gold is generally in coarse lumps, varying in value from ten cents to six hundred dollars. The largest piece we have taken out weighed $44.50. That there is a vast amount of gold still remaining in these mountains there can be no doubt. You can find it in every ravine, on the banks of every stream and even upon the side of the mountain, but not in sufficient quantities to make the collection of it profitable at present, when the expenses are so high and the facilities for working so limited. It is unevenly deposited, so that the large and rich deposits are comparatively few. Those who happen to find them (for it is all a matter of chance) will make fortunes, while thousands will accumulate but little, and many return home as poor as when they left. Great discoveries will yet be made, and I hope to be one of the favored few to make them. The mines of California will not be exhausted for many years, and those now considered unproductive will become very valuable when capital and machinery shall be combined to work them.

Should fortune favor me in the present season I shall return home in the fall. I would be satisfied with a small fortune now that the fickle goddess has played me false so often. The hardships to be endured, the dangers to be incurred, and the privations experienced are more than equal to the compensation received in nineteen cases out of twenty. The life of a miner is made up of a continued series of toil and danger. He is his own cook, wash woman, tailor, and pack horse. He rises early in the morning, cooks his scanty meal, which consists principally of pork and bread, and repairs to his labor, which is of the hardest kind. At noon he prepares himself another coarse meal and again pursues his work. At dusk he again repairs to his cabin, wearied and stiffened by toil, prepares his supply by the dim light of his cabin fire, rolls himself up in his blanket, and throwing himself upon the ground floor, dreams of heaps of gold, or of his wife and little ones at home. As he sits by the cheerful fire on his own hearth stone, the partner of his bosom glides noiselessly about in preparing his evening repast, the savory smell of which, causes his mouth to water; while his cherubs, climbing upon his knees, with their pouting lips upturned to solicit a father's kiss, and as he stoops to impress the paternal token of affection, he embraces and brings his lips in contact with his dirty blanket. Awaking, he looks around his dark cabin with a wild stare, till recollecting his present locality, he regains his sleeping posture to dream again, perhaps of the morning call of the "church going bell," the smile and looks of love, of "the girl he left behind him," the merry laugh, and the gingling bells of the sleigh with its joyous freight gliding over the smooth surface of the driven snow, or of mingling with beauty amid the mazes of the giddy dance. But this won't do. I am becoming too romantic and shall get the blue devils if I continue. Such as I have described, however, is the daily routine of the miner's occupation. Sunday is occupied in mending and washing his clothes and in cooking for the week. He is in continual danger from wild animals, savages, and difficult places in traversing the mountains through which it is necessary to pass. Mr. Horace Bucklin, a member of our company, in attempting to come from Bidwell to this place (and which he accomplished in fourteen days) suffered most severely. He subsisted for several days upon a small piece of bread, and snow; was treed by two enormous grizzly bears, where he remained all of one night, freezing his feet severely. This is not the only incident; they are of daily occurence. Had I time I would give you the particulars of some of them. Mr. Hobart and Wm. are neighbors to me. They are well and doing well, making from twelve to sixteen dollars per day. Chandler lives within sixty rods. I do not know how he is doing. Linas West, Sol Platner, Sidmore and Hasbrook are some few miles above here. They have made something, how much I am unable to say. Geo. W. Hoag is at Bidwell's attending to the duties of his office (Deputy Sheriff). Geo. B. Allcott still remains with Stout. Tho. Cook has gone to Sacramento city, and is in business of some kind. Tho. Manser is now on Nelson Creek working with Wm. Highly; Geo. Bostock is at "Tolle's diggings" doing nothing. — Henry Hahn, I think is practicing medicine in Hangtown. Geo. Ketchum is at Sacramento city, and C.A. Barton also. I have heard that Patience Cole and her father arrived safe. The health of all from Marshall is good, as near as I can learn. My own is extraordinarily so. My present weight is 175lb. My usual weight at home is from 132 to 142..

The crisis anticipated by me as I wrote you in my last has taken place. Numbers have failed in business in the cities; vast amounts of property and effects sold under the hammer, and all kinds of personal property fallen down below first cost. I am credibly informed that dry goods can be bought as cheap as in N.Y. city.

E.S. CAMP.

———◄◉►———

[June 25, 1851]   SAN FRANCISCO, May 9th, 1851.

MR. LEWIS—Again has San Francisco been visited by fire; and fearful and destructive as former conflagrations have been, this was by far more appalling than all the others combined. It originated on the south side of the Plaza, in a small building used as a paint shop, and soon the hotel formerly known as the Ward hotel was enveloped in flames. Then might have been seen upon the plaza thousands of human beings, dark and numberless masses, gazing upon the sight, whilst the firemen were combatting vigorously with the destroying element. The balcony and windows of the Union Hotel, situated on the east side of the plaza, and commanding a fine view of the fire, were filled with ladies and gentlemen, who imagined themselves in perfect security, and who were admiring, many of them for the first time in San Francisco, (for the steamer New Orleans, with a large number of passengers had arrived but a few hours before,) the excitement and awful granduer and phrenzy which attend a fire in this city. But the fire moves on, gaining in intensity and compass with fearful rapidity. The superhuman exertions of the firemen avail not to stay its progress. It has reached Sacramento street — it has crossed Kearney st. — it is sweeping both sides of Commercial and California sts. — it is making its way down Washington, Clay, Jackson, Merchant, Commercial, Sacramento and California sts. towards Montgomery st., where is is fondly hoped that the massive fire-proof brick and iron buildings will stay its career. Into these buildings many of the flying citizens are depositing what they have been enabled to save from their own burning buildings for safety. So great is the confidence in these noble buildings which for beauty, magnificence and apparent strength, rivaled the best of those in our eastern cities, that some left not only their treasures and goods of every description in them, but many who remained in their offices and rooms until retreat became almost impossible. In one instance several gentlemen remained in one of the brick buildings until their retreat was absolutely cut off. The iron doors and windows were hot, the flames crept through crevices, and thus smothered them working for their lives, and fortunately that building was saved, although neighboring brick buildings all around it and of equal capability to resist the flames were utterly destroyed! In Wells' splendid brick banking house, a building four stories high, occupied in every apartment — upon the second floor of which I had just moved my office — some twenty persons remained, of those occupying the building, and their friends, and supposed everything safe, but using water wherever there seemed to be any necessity for it. No one in the building moved anything; but the fire caught in the cellar, which was stored with liquor and other goods, through the negligence of some parties who were bringing their goods there for shelter, and who left a door in it open, through which the flames rushed like a whirlwind. The alarm was given to the parties above, and then they began their escape. But on coming to the front door they found it red hot — Montgomery street was a perfound

[147]

blaze of fire; but I believe they all escaped through windows and a side door, most of them badly but not mortally burned! My library and papers, which had been accumulating for a year and a half, and which were very valuable to me, with all my office furniture and clothing, were burned up.

The Parker House and the Empire were burned, and then the magnificent Union Hotel, having been abandoned by its inmates, was destined to destruction. It was a grand but mournful spectacle in the general ruin. The loss of that building alone and its furniture was probably not less than $200,000.

And now with but few exceptions the whole city, from Kearney st. on the west to Pike on the south and Pacific st. on the north, and beyond Battery st. on the east, is blazing! The wharves, along which buildings were erected for a mile into the bay, are on fire, and there is imminent danger that the hundreds, I may say thousands of vessels in the harbor, of all descriptions, will not escape; but fortunately they did escape, for by blowing up buildings and cutting down wharves, the fuel for the flames was withheld, leaving a divided line of ruins between the city in the bay and that upon the shore. Thus were millions upon millions of property saved; for besides the shipping itself, there are more goods in store upon vessels in the harbor than have been consumed. This fire has destroyed the beauty and pride of the city — it has ruined thousands who were *worth* their thousands, but who are now bankrupt. A universal consternation brooded over the minds of the people during the Sabbath, witnessing and feeling the awful visitation; and the inquiry was frequently made, Will our people have the ability or the inclination to rebuild and try their fortunes again, or will they abandon the city? But this is no longer a question; already several hundred houses are going up on the ruins, principally frail, but of sufficient capacity in which to transact business. Our heavy banking houses are also contracting to rebuild fire-proof buildings, and others think they can build, and will endeavor to do so this time so as to withstand the fiercest flames. The wharves will all be repaired within a week; and ere long the traces of this fire, like those of the preceeding ones, will be obliterated.

Among those who suffered by the fire was Mr. Easterly, formerly of Marshall. He, Mr. Savery and myself, with some assistance, moved his goods into the street, but there they were either entirely or mostly destroyed. His loss was not less than $7,000; but with that perserverance and energy which distinguished him, although prostrated, he is erecting a large one story wooden building on the same site his other building stood, which will enable him to have twice the facilities for doing business, so far as his store and shop are concerned, that he had before. The fire will give him many rich jobs in his line, and if he has his health I believe in six months from this time he will more than recover himself. His brother arrived in the Northerner the day after the fire.

Doubtless this fire has discouraged many. Hundreds have gone to the mines, in consequence of it, and many more will do the same, whilst others will leave the country as soon as they can get the means to do so.

You will observe by the papers that there was also connected with this fire a destruction of several lives; and yesterday several others were killed by the falling of the ruined walls of Delmonico's building! All the newspapers were burnt out except the Alta California, but most of them have already succeeded in starting again. All have suffered in this fire, either by the loss of property or the prostration of business; but in my judgment business will soon revive, and many merchants will make up by the increased prices of goods they had on shipboard, for the heavy losses they have experienced.

The new common council, which has just organized, have a momentous responsibility upon them. The city is involved in a debt of a million and a half of dollars. The greatest part of the taxable property of the city has been swept away for the present by this fire, whilst the damage sustained to the planked streets and the city property will cost a vast sum to repair.

Stockton, a fine and flourishing city on the San Joaquin, is also in ashes! Many suppose, not without reasonable grounds, that these fires were started by some of those desperate scoundrels from the British penal colonies, who infest and curst this country. A short time since, in this city, it was absolutcly dangerous for one to sit in his store or office alone in the evening, or to walk the streets, lest the slung shot might end his career. But when things came to this pass the citizens arose enmasse and demanded summary punishment; and the re-introduction at that time of the chain gang, and a few instances of summary vengeance inflicted, have had a tendency to make people more secure. It may be that they have lighted the torch of the incendiary, as the best and only means left for plunder.

Sunday, May 11. — To-day in company with Mr. Savery and the Messrs. Easterly, I took a stroll on the plank road leading to the Mission Dolores, to call upon our old friend Judge Ketchum. We found him in good health and spirits. He has nearly completed the heavy work he has had in charge for the last few months. He has acquitted himself well, and should have made, and I trust he has made, a handsome sum of money by his labors. He has had about ninety men at work for the last two weeks, and is pressing the work to its conclusion. I feel a pride and pleasure whilst walking over the well-made planked road from here to the Mission, in the reflection that it is the work of a Michigan man — of a Marshall friend — knowing that for years it will remain a monument of his industry in this land where labor brings so ample a reward, and where its dignity is so fully appreciated.

J.P.

DEAR MARY — In my letter to you of last month I mentioned, as an unusual occurrence, the open, dry and pleasant weather during the past winter and early part of spring. Since then a great change has taken place, bringing with it joy and hope to thousands in the valleys below, whose occupations consist in tilling the soil and raising stock, and disappointment, distress and famine to those who reside in the mining regions of the north.

Rain commenced falling in the valleys and snow on the mountains about two weeks since; and from that time until the present the weather has been an almost unceasing storm. The streams are much swollen, the bars flooded, and the mountains are covered with snow to the depth of from 8 to 12 feet. The result is, the cessation of mining operations, and the blocking up of the roads leading to the valley below. At the commencement of the storm, many of the miners in this region were but scantily supplied with provisions. This scanty supply has been exhausted, and starvation is staring them in the face. Many have already been driven to subsist upon sugar and coffee alone. Others have picked up the old cattle's feet that have been lying around the butcher's stand for weeks, and consumed them, while a few have for days subsisted upon barley, a small supply of which was bro't to this place for mule feed. The barley was prepared for use by roasting and grinding in a pepper mill —then made into soup or cake. – Those that have provisions are under the necessity of watching them closely, to prevent their being stolen. The small amount thrown into the market have been sold at enormous prices. Flour sells for $3 per lb. ($600 per bbl.) pork for the same, potatoes $1.50 per lb., beans $2 per lb., sugar $1,25 per lb. Hundreds have already left for settlements below, and many more are preparing to leave. Should no provisions arrive within a few days, those remaining here will resort to dog and mule meat for sustenance, until the supply here, viz: 5 dogs and 3 mules, are all consumed. What the end of this state of things will be none can tell. At present the prospect is gloomy in the extreme.

April 20. Since writing the above the storm has ceased, and a small amount of provisions have been packed upon the backs of men through the snow to relief. Efforts are being made to open a trail through for pack animals, and we anticipate a full supply of provisions within 8 or 10 days at most. The river bars are still unworkable, on account of high water. Many of the miners are in consequence out of employ. This state of affairs, however, will not continue long, as the water is rapidly falling.

April 28. The weather is clear and pleasant again. Large trains of pack animals have arrived with an abundant supply of provisions, which are sold at reasonable price. What we would consider reasonable you would undoubtedly look upon as enormous. We consider flour at $75 per bbl., pork at $100 do., sugar at 65 cts. per lb., beans at $25 per bush., potatoes at $25 do., as reasonably low. The cost at Sacramento or Marysville is trifling compared with the cost of the packing, through the snow and over the mountains to this point. The lowest price for packing is $25 per hundred pounds, and the business even at this rate is not lucrative.

The rivers and mountain streams are high, so that comparatively little can be done in mining the bars. Large numbers are in consequence leaving these diggings in search of others; hundreds have struck out for the head waters of this (Feather) river, and some have already penetrated into the mountains a distance of one hundred miles or more, north and east of this place. Reports have reached us that rich diggings have been discovered. They are however too vague to rely upon. That there will be rich discoveries made in this northern region of California, I have no doubt. Everything indicates it to be a rich and extensive gold district. The precious metal is found upon the mountains, in the valleys, and on almost every stream; but for the present it cannot be thoroughly prospected, on account of snow and high water. New diggings have been recently discovered about 25 miles north of this, on a small stream emptying into the north fork of this (Feather) river. — Judging from the reports received from there yesterday, I am inclined to think these diggings are not very extensive.

May 8. Herman, who now runs an expressline from this place to San Francisco, has just arrived, bringing with him a letter from you. He informs me that Henry Hahn is still in Hangtown practicing medicine, and doing well. G.W. Hoag is still acting in his official capacity (deputy sheriff.) How he is doing I am not informed. Geo. B. Allcott continues with his old partner, Capt. Stout, merchandising and raising stock. George has made some two or three thousand dollars, I think, if not more. Father Hobart and William still remain here. They are enjoying a good degree of health, and making something — how much I am not able to state. A.C. Parmelee is mining about twelve miles above this place on this river. Mr. Bailey of Hastings is with him. I am not informed what amount they are making. Robinson (brother-in-law) to Sidmore) met with a serious accident a short time since. While engaged in mining, a large rock rolled upon him striking him in the side, and injuring him so much as to lay him up for two weeks. He has recovered sufficiently to walk about, and will soon be sound again. Linus West, Hasbrook, Thos. Manser, and Chandler, are somewhere in the Nelson Creek mines, I have not heard from them in some time, and know nothing about their success. William Brace is in the same neighborhood, upon Poor Man's Creek. The distance from here is about forty miles. I have not heard or seen Geo. Bostock since last fall. He was then at Tolle's Diggings, 18 miles from Bidwell's Bar. He had made some two or three hundred dollars at that time. Geo. Ketchum is at San Francisco, engaged in jobbing, building a plank road leading from the city out to what is called the "Missions," a distance of two miles. He is a sub-contractor, and had about sixty thousand dollars' worth of the work to do. Patience Cole and her father are somewhere in California. They arrived safe, but I have been unable to learn at what point they located. Morgan L. Rood, from Eaton county, is here. He has probably been more successful than any other one of the "Wolverine Rangers". He has made over six thousand dollars, Herman saw Thos. Vick in Sacramento about six weeks since, but did not learn what he was doing. Dennis Cronnin was here during the first of the famine mentioned in the first part of this letter, and being somewhat alarmed at the gloomy prospect, returned to the valley. Van Brunt is mining somewhere on the Yuba. He made quite a fortune in business at Marysville, but I have been informed that he has lost a part of it by loaning and giving credit. S.B. Shepherd's brother, that used to be clerk for Wilmarth, is at Bidwell's Bar engaged in merchandising and teaming. I think he must have done well. He has done, and continues to do, a snug, safe and profitable business. Thomas E. Cook has gone to the Sandwich Islands, in company with E.D. Lord, who came over with the "Rangers," and formerly did business at Milwaukee.

I have been very particular in writing to you about all the Marshall boys, knowing that their friends are ever anxious to hear from them. — You are at liberty to have any portion of my letter published that would be on interest, or give information to others. Give my respects to all enquiring friends.

Yours, affectionately.   E.S. CAMP.

❧ ❧ ❧ ❧ ❧ ❧ ❧ ❧ ❧ ❧ ❧ ❧ ❧ ❧ ❧ ❧ ❧

487

copies printed in Linotype Caledonia on Warren's Oldstyle paper
on a 10 x 15 Chandler & Price platen press by
JOHN CUMMING
Mount Pleasant   Michigan